Life in the Park

29 humorous articles from Tammy Watson

A collection of stories published in
The Wills Point Chronicle and the Tawakoni Guide

Published by:
Helm Production
215 Laura Wilkes Rd
West Monroe, LA 71292
USA

Library of Congress Control Number:
2009939104

ISBN-13: 978-0-9842287-6-8
ISBN-10: 0-9842287-6-4

www.TammyWatson.com

Index

1 - Introduction
2 - Wrong Way Watson
6 - A Rogue By Any Other Name
9 - All's Well That Ends Well
12 - Angels Among Us
15 - Catfish Wishing
18 - Here's Your Sign
21 - It's All in the Details
24 - Jaws And Other Lake Monsters
27 - Leave It To Beavers
30 - Life's Guarantee
33 - March Madness
34 - Things 'Not to Do' in Most Every Situation
38 - Now You See It…Now You Don't
41 - It's All a Matter of Perspective
44 - The Scam Artist
47 - Stick
50 - Tempting Fate
54 - The Bad Name Bunny
56 - The Bluebird Of Happiness And Other Myths
59 - The Circus Cemetery
63 - The Gathering
66 - The One That Got Away
70 - The Trouble With Critters
73 - There is Only One Way to Test That…
77 - There Ought to be a Sign!
79 - To Do, or Die
82 - Two Weddings and a Birthday
85 - White Men Can't Dance
89 - Wood Duck Boxes, And Other Reasons Couples Fight

Introduction

Did you ever notice life is full of ironies?

When I was young I wanted to travel the world, marry a handsome prince and become a famous actress. It sounded pretty common place as far as dreams went. Then life happened.

Since marrying my husband Ken (alias handsome prince), I have traveled extensively to Paris, Italy and Athens to name a few. There is just one little problem. They are all in Texas. Not really the life plan I envisioned, but since my prince drives a white truck and protects State Parks instead of castles, it seems a close second.

Now I write stories, instead of bringing them to life on stage, which is probably a good thing. Did I mention I get terrible stage freight? Regardless, I found myself actually loving this unfamiliar, but truly rewarding change of plans. Before long, I began to naturally write down all the odd and hilarious things I saw all around me living on a State Park. Mostly thanks to people like you. Oh, and me too. Seems I am not so immune to dumb mistakes, after all. I have found, more than once, that despite knowing better...well, I get myself into a lot of situations that the first thing I think is..."Yep, this was a mistake."

So, I guess I get to be a star, after all. Only I was sort of hoping it would be walking down a red carpet, not tripping on one. Oh, well.

I hope you enjoy reading these stories of Ken and my adventures living on a State Park. Who knew, life could be so entertaining? I suppose I never did, or I would have chosen it on purpose. So, come along with us and find out why a "Life in the Park", is more fun than you could ever imagine.

Tammy Watson

P.S. You will probably notice my prince does not come save me like in the books either. Sigh. Maybe my next project should be a fairy tale about a clumsy princess who goes on adventure with her prince and saves herself. Well, sort of. At least, she survives it. Let me know what you think.

Wrong Way Watson

What a nice month I have had, how about you? I guess it was partly to do with this wonderful time of year. You step outside to find summer right around the corner, yet the cool breeze of spring seems to beckon us to drag out our camping gear and head for a fishing hole or some other distant campground. Yes, there is almost a feeling of expectation, as you head out, all self doubt seeming to have disappeared with the last frost and now you are ready for your first real adventure of the season.

Speaking of which, I really should give up the Kayaking idea.

Honestly, I can't to seem to stop myself, and it isn't as if I go down the same part of a river every time, for that matter, practice until I get really good at the sport. No siree, I just get a notion in my head to do the thing and I snatch up some rented paddles and defiantly shove off into the great unknown. Which is never a good thing, by the way. And this past month was no exception.

Ken and I had decided we needed some time away. We managed to wheedle out two days and one night. So I got right to work on the planning phase. Going to all foreign countries? Out. The mountains? Out. The beach? Out. But I was not to be deswaded. There had to be some way for me to have an adventure. Throughout this process, no matter how outlandish my ideas, Ken would simply raise an eyebrow and say nothing. He does that a lot. The eyebrow thing.

Finally I decided to make a 'quick' run to San Antonio. After all, it was only seven or so hours away. I could see it clearly, we would take in the river walk, see Sea World, and catch a museum...Ken sat up a little straighter and cleared his throat. "Tammy, we can't possibly do all that in two days." I hate when he ruins my plans with logic. So, I tried the fast talking method. Hey, it sometimes works. It didn't. However, he was by this time desperate enough to do anything besides drive clear across the state in two days.

"How about Kayaking?"

The man doesn't hold back any punches. He knows I can't resist kayaking. Which is hardly fair, but there you go. So, I crumpled up my endless scraps of odd phone numbers and headed for Broken Bow. Besides I had never done the Upper part of the river. How hard could it be?

I nearly died. Again. Sigh.

My first warning should have been when the nice man dropping us off waved goodbye, suggesting we take the middle of the waterfall when we went over it. Waterfall?! I would have asked more, but at the time the fast moving current was pulling me into a sea of boulders. Shouldn't I have a little time to reacquaint myself first with how a paddle works before being slammed into a rock and wedged on top of another? This thought barely crossed my mind before I noticed Ken being flipped out of his vehicle of demise and into the sea of boulders. Oh, this definitely was not a good thing. When he did come back up it was to wave me around. Only the sad thing was that his way seemed a lot less lethal than zigzagging through two huge rocks at breakneck speed. I admitted defeat and got out into the current and inched my way over the danger spot. Okay, not very glamorous, but I am alive.

Finally, we came to a narrower part of the river. For you novices out there, this translates as "faster current with quick turns". Apparently I am not good at fast turns either. I remember thinking as Ken fought the river before me…'This was a mistake'. Too late now, I tried to paddle my way through. Yes, me against the current. Me taking the elements on in a fight I was determined to win. That dang river side cocked me and spun my kayak around without hardly any effort at all. I hate that. Have you ever gone backwards down a rock infested super slide…let me tell you…it is not exactly fun. More like terrifying. But at least I couldn't see myself nearly dying, Ken, on the other hand, had a first row seat at the bottom of the incline. I think he is still aggravated.

And tell me this. Why is it that when you do something not exactly of your choosing and nearly kill yourself in the process whoever you are with admonishes, "Have you lost your mind? Why in the world would you go down that backwards?" Let's be honest here, there isn't really an answer to that question. Besides I still had the small waterfall to worry about.

So, how did it go? Well, let's just say…it was one of our usual uneventful trips. Not.

Thank goodness this past weekend was a little less dangerous and I still had an adventure. See, the State archaeologist came out to do a dig on the park and I got to help. You don't think Ken called him in order to get out of Scuba Diving with me do you? Naw…of course not.

But regardless, to tell you the truth, it was a lot of fun.

I learned all about shovel tests. Which consists of …digging a hole to find a hole to dig. Are you confused yet? I also learned how to read a compass. Never mind that I had an orienteering class years ago. I guess I never really got the compass thing. Which is probably why when I actually took our girls orienteering with one tied around my neck, we got a little turned around…okay…lost. But now I think I could do it without getting 'turned' around. The girls said as long as it isn't with them. Now is that nice?

Anyway, back to my adventure. Ken and I got to do a small dig…with supervision. Make a graph and bag our treasure…with supervision. And then I even got to take pictures for the archaeologist…without supervision. This part worries me a bit. I think I should have brought my reading glasses because I have absolutely no idea what the pictures look like. I really think they need to make a bigger screen for those of us over forty. But then again where is the surprise in that, right? The archaeologist looked a little worried himself when I informed him of that fact. Not to mention the camera closed itself up and decided to call it a day. Funny. I guess even the camera was worried.

Ken asked why I kept taking pictures if I couldn't see them. I don't know. It probably has a lot to with the same reason why I would kayak over a small waterfall. If you figure it out, PLEASE let me know.

A Rogue By Any Other Name

Do you ever wonder why whenever some animal goes ballistic; the scientists call him a 'rogue?'

I do.

Especially since the definition for 'rogue' is; "a mischievous person." This definition hardly describes the picture Ken's office manager showed me last week. It was a little throat catching. There before my eyes hung a British navel officer dangling from a rope ladder.

Helicopter low over the water, swirling the seas around as two other officers watched from the purple waters below. Then horror of horrors, a giant great white shark was sailing through the air right at him.

I told Ken, imagine being that man, his hands frozen in terror to the ladder rung. He said, "That's nothing. Imagine being the other two still left in the water."

He had a point.

The scientists always try to comfort us at times like these with such gentle words as 'rogue.' Reminding us of the other thousands of sharks who have never bothered a soul. But, the rest of us who have ever wandered across any of these deviant critters know differently.

And it hardly matters what you call them over one shoulder, as your running for your life. Not a thing comforts you at that precise moment. And to be honest, you don't really care a whole lot about the other thousand. No siree. Not a thing.

Not too long ago a man we know told a hilarious story of one little skunk hanging around his house. Now some of you might think "big deal." But, then again it's not your house is it?

The bad thing about skunks is not knowing when they will strike. Spraying you with sweet smelling perfume, and then leaving you gagging and rolling around on the ground as they sashay off into the bushes. And then there is the rabies idea.

Not a good thing. So, living out in the boondocks he decided to end the guessing game and just shoot the thing. Only he missed. And, you know, skunks don't really like people shooting at them. A nice normal skunk would have run for the hills, but unfortunately this one wasn't-normal, that is.

Nope, he was a rogue. He turned right at the man and started running. The man turned tail and ran as well, shooting furiously over one shoulder at the demented creature. It chased him clean up the stairs and right up to the door. And thankfully, no matter how crazed, a skunk can't break down a door. It's a fact.

And then there was the time a woman had a visitor up in her attic. A nice little raccoon. Let's just call him Lucifer for short…she did. He kept her awake, tore at her ceiling and created havoc in her life.

She tried everything, traps, sealing up holes, but he always found a way in, each time getting more and more out of control. It was war. So, she called in reinforcements. Nothing worked. Even standing outside the gaping hole of her house. Waiting. Shotgun in hand. Not intimidated in the least, the raccoon simply meandered out another way. Now, that's a rogue.

Another friend of mine said a crazy stray cat started hanging out at her place. Notice she didn't put it nicely. She claims he was out to get them. He strung out their trash, picked fights with other cats under their bedroom window and terrorized her children.

The faster they ran, the more fun the game. So, after several sleepless nights, her husband had had enough. He put on his camouflage and stalked out into the night after cat. He missed. But, boy was that cat mad about the whole thing.

The next night as they sat peacefully watching television, they heard an awful, spine-jerking screech. It was the CAT. The thing was clawing at their door, throwing himself against it and carrying on for several seconds. To tell the truth, they were a little afraid to open that door. But, finally they gathered their courage and did, only to find bits of hair and cat leavings on their porch. That was the last time they ever saw him. At least, they hope so.

So far, at the park, I haven't seen many rogues. Of the animal kind anyway. Too many people, I guess. Still if you ever do run across one of these, exception to the rule critters...do what the rest of us nice normal folk do. Try to settle your differences peacefully. And if it can't be done?

Well...don't call me. I can out run you.

All's Well That Ends Well

Sometimes things just don't go the way we plan. Try as we might it just isn't in the cards...not our day...or as some like to say, "It is like a little dark cloud hovers over our head". Waiting to rain, not only on our parade, but on our whole existence. Trouble.

Well, apparently I am not alone. Take the Adventurers.

They must have read my article about how to get lost in the woods without really trying. Because boy did they manage to hit nearly every suggestion I gave. Pretty impressive.

First the two cousins decided to hike at sunset. Which is really not their fault. Sun rays shifting through tree branches is both enticing and seductive. Better to lure you in my dear. But, not taking a flashlight? Definitely their fault. Wearing dark clothes and avoiding neon colored hair? Again, their fault. And definitely making it more challenging to spot them along the trails shadowy depths.

They started on their 'hike' at seven. By ten that night their family was truly worried. But, I noticed, not worried enough to sacrifice their own bodies to the creatures of the night. Smart. Nope, they asked us to help find them. Translated: Better you than me.

As Ken and I strapped on flashlights and light jackets, thinking this would not take long, the trails are pretty short, they cleared their voice and mentioned as an afterthought, "Oh, and the boy likes excitement." This translates: Does not stay on trail. Ever.

Ken being the rational soul he is, calmly switched off his light. And told me to use my flashlight only if I truly needed it. In other words, this may take awhile. And it did. In fact we never did find those elusive kids. And the woods are not that big. Nor do the animals have a beam of light shooting through the darkness, or shout names until they are hoarse. Hmmm. Anyway, they finally showed back up at the camp around midnight. They were wore out, dog tired, and big eyed, but alive.

When asked how they found their way home? They said proudly, "Hacked our way out through the brush". In other words, just plain lucked out, after walking around in circles for five hours. Oh, well. At least they experienced an adventure and we got to practice our rescue skills.

It must be in the air. This, getting into trouble without really trying, thing. Take the "Philosophers".

A group of young Christian men who meet every week around a campfire and solve the worlds' problems. They talk for hours and encourage each other. Sounds good. Or it was until they decided to be a bit more inventive about their meetings.

They decided that if on the ground was nice. On the roof was inspiring. So, they tore down their small makeshift fireplace and hauled it up on the roof of their house one night. More atmosphere, you see. The stars twinkled overhead, the warm flames from the fireplace crackled soothingly. The boys settled down for their deep discussion, snuggled up in soft warm jackets. It was then they noticed an odd commotion going on down the street from them. Police, ambulance and fire trucks were blazing down the road, heading straight...they sat up a little straighter to see what the emergency was...then leapt to their feet as all three vechicles screeched to a stop...right in their driveway. It seems they were the emergency.

Neighbors filed out of houses. Outside lights switched on creating a sort of surreal circus attraction. And the boys? What did they say to all this? What any sane person would, seeing strangely clad men pulling a heavy hose off the strobe lighted vehicle.

"Hey, don't turn that thing on! We're up here?" There is nothing so daunting to a good discussion then getting shot off the roof by a super sized water hose. It ruins the whole ambiance. Believe me.

And my own little dark cloud? Well, the other day a pile of ladybugs descended on my house. They covered my hair, went down my shirt and even flew at my face. I hear tell they are supposed to be good luck. I certainly hope so. If not, I'm in big trouble.

Angels Among Us

Sorry about not writing last month, but being as it was filled with a few of life's little surprises (the flu being one), I found out sometimes you just have to throw your hands up and surrender for a moment. Last month was mine. Still, in amongst it all I found out that in those dark moments lay some really nice ones as well. As the saying goes "there are angels among us."

Take the flu for instance; it was brought to me by two little angels…my granddaughters. I didn't thank them for their early Christmas present and personally I no longer feel guilty about the Asparagus incident either. I figure we are even now. Oh? And I suppose you have never tried to sneak some golden vegetable past a young ones eyes. Hah! Well, it nearly worked. See, I made this wonderful dinner for them (perhaps it was a little on the burnt side) and doctored up some asparagus for her to try. As I happily watched from the kitchen, she took one bite, screwed up her face in obvious distaste and shoved the limp vegetable at Ken. And with true southern diplomacy she confided, "Papa, this needs some sauce, or sugar or something." Ken thought it needed more that that. He is still laughing. Sigh. As least my angels brought laughter with the flu.

Then my dog nearly died. As much as I complain about the silly thing, I am deeply attached. So, Ken toted her off to the dog hospital, much against his better judgment and some angels worked their magic and saved her. I knew she was getting better when Ken tried to give her a pill. He argued with the dumb dog for five minutes, before shoving it down her throat, closing her mouth, massaging her throat and daring her to defy him. She calmly looked him straight in the eye and then when he let go? Spit it clear across the room. He still swears she gave a smug smile afterwards. Ken says it certainly wasn't 'his' angels that saved her, that's for sure. But, they were mine.

Why I even got to be an angel of sorts this past month. Ken and I were checking the trails when we happened across a GeoCacher (treasure hunt with GPS). We have like three treasures buried on the park by this group who use their GPS to hunt down said treasures, root them out and then replace them back into their hiding place. Sounds fun, but…well, as far as I can tell it isn't finding them that is the trouble. Nope, it seems these technical people don't have a bit of trouble with that part. It is getting back out of the woods that stump them. See, our park is like one of those fancy English mazes. It looks pretty easy and you get thinking that maybe, just maybe you can beat the odds and figure the way out yourself. Only most times? Well, you can't. And believe me those GPS gadgets are no help whatsoever if you don't know where you are to begin with. Trouble.

Anyway, this lady was the friendly sort and kept looking longingly at our mule (what we call the little truck), the whole time we explained to her the way out. Rather than taking off, she kept mentioning how long she had been walking, her cell phone was nearly dead and people must be worried and…Hey, I can take a hint. We scooted over and drove her out of the wilderness. I think she was so grateful she would have hugged us if she wouldn't have been clutching her gadgets so tightly.

Well, I hope you had your share of angels this last year. I know I certainly have. I think that is what makes this life wonderful. Real, caring people. Mikea told me of one of her angels. She has to go to work early in the morning, (how one can call dark thirty morning is beyond me), and walk across a dark parking lot. In the winter it is cold, dark and scary. One day she was praying God send one of His angels to watch over her and she looked over and an older customer from her store happened to get out of his car at the same time. He usually came in a lot later, but relieved to have company she waved, he waved and they walked a distance apart to work.

The next morning he was there again. Odd. This kept happening all week. My family is a little on the slow side, but finally Mikea stopped and turned around, asking, "Are you coming here early every day just to walk me to work?" He blushed before nodding. "I have a granddaughter your age and I would hope if someone saw her walking across a dark parking lot they would watch over her too." With a teary smile Mikea thanked him and securely walks to work every morning knowing her angel is there with her.

I think that will be my New Year's resolution this year. To not let any 'angel' moments past me by. How about you?

Catfish Wishing

I think there are two kinds of fishing.

There is catching. And then there is wishing. Sadly, I fall under the wishing sort, especially when it comes to those sneaky catfish. I've about decided you have to get a "feel" for them.

A lot like making my Granny's biscuits. Doesn't matter if you have the recipe and she was sitting right there beside you. They still will come out hard on the outside and doughy on the inside if you don't have the touch. And I...most definitely...do not when it comes to catching.

No don't even start with how easy it is either. Believe me, I've asked any and every soul I've seen with a fish dangling off the other end of a pole and I've about decided this is not an exact science. In fact, I'm beginning to wonder if people just tell you crazy things to keep you busy while they catch all the fish.

For example, Ken's grandmother swore up and down the cows knew. If they were laying down the fishing was bad.

Last time I checked cows don't even associate with fish. I know this for a fact. After all, I'm a fairly intelligent individual. Yet, when it comes to fishing, something weird happens to my brain and I will try just about anything. So, if I see even one cow lying down. I shake my head sadly and say, like I'm an expert, "Not any use fishing today."

A few weeks ago, I was fishing as usual, and looked up from my book-(Hey, I have to do something to keep from yanking my pole up every five seconds)-anyway, when I heard someone say something about spitting on a worm.

Apparently, your suppose to take some chewing tobacco and then spit on your poor mangled worm. Then, presto, you catch a fish. Yuck. You would never in a million years catch me doing something disgusting like that. No Siree. I have some pride after all.

So…I waited until everyone else went back to their respective poles, drug, in my drowned worm and spit upon it. Twice. I figured since I didn't have any tobacco I needed to do something for an added gesture. Did I catch a fish? Of course not.

So, I am left with scavenger fishing. You know my sort. If someone leaves a spot, I run over and set up my chair. If they are catching fish, I ask what they were using for bait.

And if I am especially desperate I will ask someone to let me see the length from their hook to the bobber. Yes, I have to use a bobber, even with catfish. But, I prefer to think of the bobber as a training wheel of sorts.

To help me along until I get the "feel." I did this a few weeks ago and longingly looked off two chairs away while people effortlessly pulled in 27 catfish.

Toward the end they were swearing they would stop after the next one. Meanwhile I watched my floating bobber stay depressingly peaceful upon the water.

There was one think I hadn't tried yet. The wind thing. A kind man told me to try fishing in the wind. And it even had a logical ring to it. So, a couple of days later Ken and I went for a relaxing stroll to the water. We climbed up on the picnic table and suddenly something caught our eye. Yep, people were catching.

I ran up, asking what kind of bait and the length thing. I had to hurry, the sun was starting to set. Then we raced back grabbing up our poles and fishing gear. The sky was turning colors now, the pressure was on.

Reaching the point we quickly snatched a good spot still warm from the previous owners and checked for wind. Then I threw my line in and …wonder of wonders…I caught a catfish. It was the most beautiful thing I ever saw.

Never mind that the other guys at the end of the point caught a three pounder and no telling what else on totally different bait. But, I didn't care. Not one little bit. I wasn't jealous at all.

Okay-maybe just a little.

Here's Your Sign

Did you know you can't go camping in a graveyard?

Well, it's true. At least according to a sign hanging off the chain link fence in a certain small west Texas town. Now, I don't know about you, but personally the notion never struck me. Not once.

So, I couldn't stop laughing. Turns out a poor man who was never quite right, lost one of his family members. To be near them, he started taking his sleeping bag out to the graveyard. No one minded at first. That is until a rather well off family went out to plan funeral services.

For some reason, they thought he might be a bit of a distraction to the whole process. When they went to complain to the sheriff, he said, "Can't do anything about it. There isn't a sign saying you can't camp in a graveyard."

Needless to say, they went to the courthouse and got a sign.

Seems like to me there are a lot of signs out there I once thought were...well...dumb. But, it turns out if it's on a sign, someone tried to do it. Take for instance, the small sign when you drive into Huntsville State Park. It states, 'Do not feed the alligators.'

That seems like a pretty obvious thing to me. But then again, I don't like to flirt with danger. Especially if danger has big yellow sharp teeth and is twice my size. Apparently some people do.

Park rangers had to stop one lady from feeding an alligator popcorn. She never seemed to notice it waddling up a little closer each time she reached down for another handful. Now most people aren't aware of it, but an alligator can run. Anyway, the park ranger calmly asked her a very thought provoking question. "What happens when you run out of popcorn?"

She stopped feeding the alligator.

Living at a state park, we have signs. A lot of them. Which means somewhere, sometime…someone has done something that needed a sign. Take the, 'no boats within 200 feet of this sign,' near the swimming area. It is to keep jet skis and other boats from running over the little children frolicking unaware in the swimming area.

Ken has caught people tying their boat to it. I guess it's handy. I told Ken maybe if he removed the sign they wouldn't have anything to tie their boat to…he said…we need the sign. I know, we could get a sign that says no tying your boat to the 'no boats within 200 feet'one.

Hey, it's an idea.

Apparently, we aren't the only ones with sign trouble. Last week Ken and I went diving at a place close to Terrell. We were telling him all about our sign trouble when he motioned towards a dock. "Did you notice my signs?" Do I dare admit I didn't?

Ken was nodding. He notices things like signs. Something to do with his job. Anyway, it turns out the owner was having trouble with people leaving their gear all over the dock. This is not a good thing. See, divers have a big, heavy pressurized air tank attached to their back.

Falling with a big heavy tank of air slamming into your back or the dock as you trip over said gear…not a pretty picture. So, he got – a sign. They were fairly expensive and worded politely. 'Please do not leave unattended gear on the dock.'

The next week there must have been 300 pieces of gear – on the dock. But, only three men standing around. I guess they were 'attending.' He asked politely if they read the sign. They said they did; only they didn't really understand it. He didn't say a think, but walked off and found a can of red spray paint. He then preceded to mark through the words 'Please' and 'unattended.' It now reads, 'do not leave your gear on the dock.' It worked. And so another sign was born.

I guess there will always be rules and signs for people. It's like the infamous 'they' of the world think we don't have any common sense at all. For instance, did you know the state has a rule; 'Spouses cannot work together at the same park.'
Well…yeah. So, where's my sign?

It's All in the Details

There are a lot of things in life that are amusing in a ridiculous sort of way. We make fun of people all the time because of them. Take the Darwin awards, superstitions, dating and even our own curiosity. Over the years I have discovered that what makes nearly everything funny is rather than walk away from a certain situation, someone, somewhere said, "I believe I can just wing it. After all how hard can it be?" Never a good idea – winging it.

Take dating. In of itself a perfectly harmless little exercise. That is except when you decide to try and jazz it up a bit by going on the internet. Then it becomes something else entirely. Personally I have too many trust issues to believe anyone I can't look in the eyes. Besides there is a certain kind of day dreamy trance that comes over people and suddenly a five foot computer geek becomes...poof...a tall handsome football player. This would be fine so long as they never met. Unfortunately, it is hard to date without actually dating. Therein lies the problem. Do you tell your potentially significant other the truth, or hope they won't notice the height difference? Well, you say if they really liked me that little detail would hardly matter...hmmm...

A couple of weeks ago one of the park rangers told me a man came into the park spitting mad. Okay, maybe he wasn't spitting, but he was in a tizzy, as my grandmother use to say. Seems he was supposed to have this romantic interlude with a woman he had met on the internet, at our park, none the less. Only on the way down, he got a call about five minutes before they were supposed to meet. Seems she had decided to come clean with a few minor details she might have forgotten to mention. The biggest being she was a little, how do you say? Oh, yes – married. That might have been important to know before he drove hours to get here. I guess the saying, "it's all in the details", is true. Well, at least as far as internet dating goes.

I have probably already mentioned it but I was raised by a rather superstitious grandfather. You scoff, but tell me how many times have you "knocked on wood"? Or how about, having your heart race as you defiantly cross a black cat's path. Ridiculous as they sound, there is only one way to test if their real or not, and personally I don't care to take a chance on seven years bad luck. I barely can get through one day. Anyway, there are a couple of park hosts who come from Louisiana and although they claim their not superstitious they have met quite a few who are. It must be that Cajun influence. One man topped them all. If he saw a black cat, he would get out draw an 'X' on the pavement with his finger, spit and then climb back into his car and head the opposite direction. Which I have to say, aggravates me somewhat. I mean, now I not only have to turn around, but I have to draw that durn 'X' and spit first. I imagine people will give me awfully strange looks when I do it too. The way I figure it, most people don't know about the 'X' and spitting part. Regardless of the fact that I have never actually been told what exactly happens if you cross that path without all the hoopla, and mind you, nothing at all might, well…that little detail just might make or break the whole black cat thing. So, I guess I'll just have to keep making 'X's.

Ken's brother had a story of his own. He said, that on the land his boss owned, were all these mortar rounds (little bombs that airplanes drop), for those girls who like me had no idea there was difference in bombs. Anyway, what they were doing scattered about no one had any idea, but Ken's brother decided he would let them lie until the bomb squad got there. Turns out that was a wise decision.

Come to find out there was someone else once who found a working bomb (Excuse me, mortar round). It was discovered exposed at the edge of the water lying peaceably in the mud minding its own business. And being as it looked pretty old (We're talking World War II), the bomb squad wasn't that concerned. After all how active could it be if it had been lying there all this time? So, they put on one of those little charge, thing-a-ma-gigs, that punch holes in metal and took cover behind this makeshift protection. But when the charge went off, all they heard was this little dink sound, like metal hitting metal. Disappointed, they went over to have a look.

Walking over, they noticed there was barely a dent in it. So being boys, they decided that if one charger only dinked it a bit, then three charges would definitely do the trick. So, laughing and talking, they casually placed three charges on top and ambled back towards the cover. Not really that eventful as far as bomb squad days go.

However, they barely made it back behind the cover when something unexpected happened.

A huge explosion. So loud that it made them all throw their arms up over their heads in self defense. Parts of nearby tree stumps exploded and went sailing overhead as mud rained down on the shocked Bomb squad. When they finally looked up, it was to see a ten foot deep hole gaping before them where a mortar round had been. Seems even old bombs stuck in the mud for years actually blow up when provoked.

And the next time they find an old bomb? Definitely only two charges! Apparently, especially where bombs are concerned anyway...it's all in the details.

Jaws And Other Lake Monsters

In case you haven't noticed – this is one big lake.

Living here watching the lake change with the seasons, I am constantly reminded of the ocean. Especially when a storm is brewing overhead and the waves grow larger and more intense.

It is a little overwhelming at times. I agree with my nephew from Kansas, who upon seeing the ocean for the first time, reached up and solemnly grabbed hold of his mother's hand. He refused to budge, pointing out into the oceans endless depths. "I could get lost out there."

He had a point.

Anything bigger than we are sets our hearts to racing and our imagination to churning. Especially, if the said body of water is murky and full of strange splashes beside your head. It's a little unnerving. You think…I am not alone out here and I'm not sure I like the company.

You remember fabled stories of Lock Ness monsters, Jaws, body crushing snakes and alligators. Now, you know realistically, those are just stories. But, it's hard to convince the irrational part of your brain that is frantically looking around for an escape route.

Even as I write, three kids have stopped dead in their tracks to peer into the water. They see something strange. Curious they debate what exactly it is…and nobody wants to reach their hand down and find out. They start the – "I'm not going to touch it, you touch it" – game.

Finally, the boy braves up enough to check it out. They all laugh. It is only odd colored sand. And so they creep out a little farther into the swimming area. Watchful.

Even my grown son-in-law is not immune. He stands six foot four and counting. Weighs around 200 and plenty of muscle to go along with it. Yet, many an imagination has felled bigger men than he.

And so my story begins.

We had a house full of company. People everywhere, flowing in and out of my small house. So, as sunset approached everyone went for hikes and a few headed down for the swimming beach. It's beautiful and fairly empty at this time of day. The sky grew full of pinks and blues, reflecting off the calm surface of the water. Yes sir. Peaceful and serene.

From the shore.

Most of us were burying each other's feet in the sand and jumping out. We felt fairly safe. After all, sea monsters can't come onto the shore – it's a rule. Anyway, my son-in-law and daughters grew braver as dusk approached. They egged each other out into the darkening water.

I tried not to watch. Soon they were waist deep and splashing each other with cool water. Still, they went deeper. Then I heard it.

A bloodcurdling scream. As I looked up all three kids were pushing the water aside, frantically racing for the safety of shore. They were shouting and laughing at the same time. You know, that delirious laughter you see the actor make when he things he is safe, right before he is swallowed up by a horrible creature of the deep. It was kinda like that.

They were running now, looking back over their shoulders...my son-in-law shoving my daughters ahead of him through the water. The guys always sacrifice themselves in the movies. And me? Well, I acted like a true spectator. I shouted back inane things like..."Big fish?" and "I don't see anything"...from the safety of shore.

But, did we go try to save them? Of course not. I'm not crazy. That is why I stayed on shore happily burying my other daughter's feet. I did encourage them to run father though. Does that count?

By the time they reached shore they were all talking at once. Something about a big giant fish chasing them out of the water. I raised an eyebrow. Really. Everyone knows big fish don't chase people. Leave it to the imagination of 20 year-olds.

A few days later I was riding by the swimming area and a huge fish slowly rolled out of the water and back down again. I started breathing again and high tailed it out of there. Ken says it was just a large carp. I guess. I mean, you and I both know there are no man-eating fish in the lake. Right?

Leave It To Beavers

I think it is amazing how even God's smallest creatures have personalities. And living here at the park I have seen so many funny critters and their ways.

Take for instance the black squirrels. Oh, they fool you with their cute little faces and furry tails. I remember when we first moved here and they would boldly stay right in your path, daring you, with the big truck, to do something about it besides honk. Then, when they were finished with whatever it is squirrels do in the middle of the road, they would amble off. Honestly, they acted as if they were here first or something.

Now most of the other critters were not so bold. The deer stayed out of sight. Deer are normally shy like that. Some birds tried to threaten from the skies, but were mostly all chirp. And the stray dogs soon learned to break park leash laws by sneaking around at night. They got tired of going off to doggie jail and warned their friends as well.

But, the beavers made me laugh the hardest.

See, I just never knew beavers had gourmet taste. You would think when it came to tree chomping they were pretty much the same. After all, how picky would a beaver really be? Apparently, very.

Let me start at the beginning.

When we moved here, the park hosts told us of a place where a beaver dam existed. Cool. And even though I went out to observe the average size dam several times and never saw one beaver, I could tell they were around. There were the occasional tracks and cut down trees to prove their existence. So, I figured we don't bother them and they don't bother us. Boy, did I not understand beavers and their love of trees.

Shortly after we finished the dock, the engineers decided we needed some native trees to slow down the erosion of the "Point." The Point is a piece of land here that juts out into the water between the swimming hole and the boat dock. It is one of the prettiest spots to sit and is covered in new green grass, with a rock shoreline around it. But, in order to help preserve it, we needed trees. So, they ordered 90 black willow trees. It took two days to get them all in place. Young, sturdy trees, all neatly moving in the breeze.

It took the beavers exactly one week to clear the land of them.

Now at first we thought the beavers would just chop down a few and move on. Were we ever wrong. The first morning after they were planted, only 70 remained. Soon it was 60...40...and finally a mere six, on closer inspection we discovered one to have a section cut clean through the middle and left hanging there, tied neatly to the post. Why exactly, we weren't sure. Maybe it was the beaver's way of leaving us a warning. More trees or else.

Now even a true naturalist will have to admit there is no sharing with someone who takes 84 and leaves you six. Nope. It was plain old thievery. Pure and simple, apparently, beavers love black willow trees and don't intend to share. In fact, the only reason they left the six, that we could determine, was that they were under the streetlight.

Yet, in spite of carting off nearly every last tree, two weeks later we found...yep-beaver tracks circling what was left of those poor beautiful trees. Now, I don't know what they were hoping to find there. Maybe they actually believed we would be dumb enough to plant more. But, I suppose once an addict, always an addict. They had to have one last look.

Recently, we had to plant four trees across the Point to stop people from driving onto the grass. Only this time we planted wild plum trees. And you will never believe it, but those silly beavers didn't even nibble on one of them.

I suppose the moral of this story, if there were one for beavers, would he "never eat up all your willow in one week."
Oh, by the way, Ken just came in and told me…we are down to five willow trees. Sigh.

Life's Guarantee

Have you ever felt absolutely certain about something? Preached it. Embraced it. Even thought the rest of the world was just blind and deaf not to feel the same? Me too. Especially when I was in my twenties and thought I knew everything. Boy, what I wouldn't give to feel like that again. Unfortunately the older I get, well the less sure I am of a lot of things. I suppose it comes with age. Wisdom and all that. Or it could be simply that after this much time on earth you realize things are not always what they seem. And just owning up to the fact gives you the ability to step back and take another look at a situation. It comes in handy sometimes.

I'm sure my sister wished she had done that very same thing years ago. Let me set this story up for you a bit. It is late (Dark thirty, as Ken likes to call it), her husband is working the night shift and she has two babies asleep in the car. She feels a little spooked on this dark moonless night. Not to mention that she lives on a street that is…how do I put this? Not the safest in town.

Pulling up at the bottom of her launch pad…oh, did I forget to mention her driveway resembles one? An older woman once told me she needed a pulley to just get up to the front door. All that being aside, her driveway is the reason she can't shut her engine off and race for the door. And probably the reason she had time to notice the man in her house! Her heart racing and her palms sweaty she froze in indecision. Now what? There he sat as cool as a cucumber, his shadowy form rocking back and forth in her rocking chair, totally oblivious to the hallway's faint light illuminating him. It was his blatant disregard of her fear that prompted her to act. She was not going in there alone. So, armed with her new fangled cell phone she dialed the police and whispered in it for help. Meanwhile, the man rocked unperturbed back and forth in her window.

Soon two police cars screeched to a stop beside her and guns drawn, climbed up her hill and into the house. She waited down below nervously biting at her fingernails. Before long they motioned her up the hill and inside. They said someone must have ransacked her house, toys and clothes were scattered everywhere. She blushed and said rather meekly, "My family ransacked it. It was this way when I left for work." Confusion now on their faces, one of the officers put up his gun and grinned before calmly going over to the rocking chair and asking, "Is this your burglar?"

Embarrassed now beyond belief she simply nodded as he untied her child's helium balloon from the arm of the rocking chair and handed it to her. If only she had waited a little longer the 'burglar' might have deflated, and not scared her half to death. As I said, sometimes things are not always as they seem.

One of our Park Host was having a terrible month of things being not quite what they seem. She called it bad luck, but I don't know. I think that if just one had taken another look her month might not have gone quite so bad. First there were the two rows of okra she planted, nurtured, watered. Her mother, after noticing something unfamiliar growing in her garden, promptly weeded every last okra plant out of there. Not really that helpful, but if they had been weeds? Well, the Park Host might have thanked her instead of mumbling for two weeks straight about all her hard work down the tubes. Then she had car trouble. A water pump went out and one brand new tire went flat. When she walked to the 'tire' shop in the small town where it occurred, the rather inept man sipping coffee informed her he couldn't leave his 'tire shop' and she would have to drive on the flat to him. Which I am sure would not have been near as aggravating had he actually been in his tire shop at the time, instead of a coffee shop when he told her this. Never the less, she dutifully walked back and drove her car to the 'tire shop' only to have him admit matter of factly, "Well, now I don't actually have any tires, but for a price I can sure put that little doughnut tire on for you."

Now see, if she hadn't had a false impression, she would have been perfectly fine with the tire change, but she rather expected to find a tire to be in a tire shop. Her mistake. What can I say? Life has no guarantees after all.

So, now it's summer here at the Park. Campers are rolling in. Some are cheerful and some kind of grumpy from their long rides in, but the one thing they share is an expectation of sorts about what they 'think' a camping vacation will consist of. And I can nearly guarantee they won't consider sunburns, mosquitoes, bugs or heat in the equation. And I also know for a fact that if they roll in with thunder rolling in the background and lightening flashing as raindrops fall on their windshields and they ask if it's going to rain? Well, I simply shake my head and say..."In life there are hardly any guarantees."

March Madness

Wow, what a crazy month it has been. There must have been something in the air because March seemed wrought with weird instances of temporary…well, insanity.

I should have known something was up when an omen came in the guise of a fish. A few of weeks ago I walked up on a small group of park hosts gathered around this fisherman and his unusual catch. After explaining just how unusual, (as in the fish hatchery people where coming to take it away) kind of unusual, he proudly hauled it up to reveal this beautiful Holsten (white bellied with a black back) catfish. I have to admit it was pretty impressive dangling there before me, all sleek and colored up like that, but looking back I should have realized…it was a sign of even stranger things to come…of impending doom…of…okay, maybe not doom, but certainly a few perplexing moments to be sure.

Things 'Not to Do' in Most Every Situation

Have you ever wished there existed a list out there of really bad ideas?

Oh, not so you would do them. But rather so you could avoid doing them. Because believe me, if the person who first invented Bungi jumping had had a list, and in a that moment of insanity when he thought, "You know it might be a good thing to tie a rope to my ankle and jump off this bridge. Not only that but make sure I fall upside down, so as it eliminate any chance of survival. Who knows, it might be fun?" Then I guarantee that if there had been a list, then at least one rational human being would have held up a finger in protest, suggesting wisely, "I don't know, that sounds a little...well...insane. Why don't we check the list?"

On it we would have found our mother's words, "And I suppose if all your friends jumped off a bridge you would too?"

Only there was no list. And because of it, sadly enough everyone now can answer yes to that question. They would jump off a bridge with their friends. Not only yes, but enthusiastically pay thirty dollars a piece for the privilege. So, personally I think we need a list.

Take the movie, "Dirty Dancing". Through the years it has probably crossed many a viewers mind, "I could do that". No problem. How hard can it be? Well...let's just say...such thoughts definitely need to be on the list. My youngest daughter Mikea and her friend Ryan decided one hot summer day to put the theory to the test. After all, he was a pretty big guy. And if lean Patrick Swayze could fling a girl about effortlessly, so could he. All needed to he manage the feat was one willing partner. (Perferably a very small one) And one swimming pool. Did I mention they are college educated? After all, there was still the chance they could be wrong. Hence the swimming pool, which would break their fall.

All bases covered, Ryan steeled himself for the big moment. Now all he would have to do is lift said girl (Mikea) high over his head in triumph. Sounded good in theory. But the problem is, most girls have trust issues about being flung in the air, then balanced overhead on trembling arms. No matter the guy. And that Ryan did it at warp speed didn't help matters.

So how did it turn out? Well, let's just say it was a knee jerk experience. He did the flinging and she did the knee jerking – right into his eye knocking him nearly unconscious. All I can say is - they certainly don't show you that part in the movies.

Then there is the seemingly benign Biology class. There you are constantly asked to memorize and repeat back. Generally when one is in uncharted territory, humans trust their professors to lead them down the road of learning. Only sometimes the road of learning seems a little strange. It is at these times…I suggest you check your list.

Unfortunately my sister's friend didn't have a list. So, one day exhausted from work, children and school she dragged herself to class. Plopped down on one of those tall hard round stools and waited. Prying her eyes open she tried to concentrate on every word of instruction. It was the unfamiliar procedure of how to dissect a cat. Not a pleasant experience to say the least. Let's see. Open package. Observe various cat parts thoroughly. Pour on solution. Rewrap. And, oh yes. Don't forget to shake it.

She raised an eyebrow. But on observing that no one else seemed the least bit queasy about the process, she gave a wan smile and began. She opened, looked, poured, rewrapped and finally -- shook. The dead cat.

She knew immediately this was wrong. For one, there were the football players across from her. They were laughing so hard they couldn't even catch their breath. Then there was the way everyone else was staring at her in horror. Not a good thing.

Embarrassed, she gingerly laid down the cat and tried to ignore the rude laughter coming from across the table. Come to find out, it was the solution she was supposed to shake. Not the poor cat. See? She needed that list. The shaking of dead cats would have definitely been on it.

Campers also are in need of a list. Especially in the summer. Because when people get hot, they start getting desperate. And believe me, in East Texas it can get hot. Hot enough to melt the tar off the road and onto your shoes kind of hot.

The other day it was just that hot. People covered the beaches, hoping for a breath of cool air off the water. Other brave souls ventured out into the lake's depths for relief. And others? Well, they thought of a more original approach.

Ken first knew something was not right when the breaker for a big portion of campers kept going off. They would fix it. It would flip back off. They would fix it...you get the picture. Finally Ken decided to go from camper to camper and find out what was causing the overload. It was then he discovered the thick hundred-foot extension cord leading from an outlet, across the road and into the woods. Like the real detective he is, he followed the suspicious line. And what he found? Well, let's just say, what he found made him speechless.

For there before him sat one Speedo clad man slumped down in a lawn chair all spread out in front of this huge air conditioner. It was blowing cold air straight at the man and doing it's level best to cool off the entire park as well. Unfortunately, it was failing miserably. So, by the time Ken found his voice, it was a low roar. The man, however, seemed totally obvious as to why it presented such a problem. Let's just say, 'Ken pulled the plug on that little idea.'

So the next time a brilliant, if slightly strange inspiration overtakes you, remember to check the list. It might be another dead cat.

Now You See It...Now You Don't

Life is a little like a magic show sometimes. Oh, and your in the audience and get called up on stage. Yep, at first you fluctuate between elated, embarrassed, and even somewhat apprehensive. I mean, there you are shifting nervously readjusting your clothing, running your tongue over your teeth to check for lipstick smears and the whole time all your frantic mind can think is, "Oh my gosh. Oh my gosh." Which translates into "Have I lost my ever loving mind?" There is no answer to this question.

Perhaps we feel like we can handle most things. Life, magic, it is all pretty much the same thing right? So what if we have never actually disappeared before, or been sawed in two. We somehow convince ourselves that we are perfectly capable of taking care of the situation. Or, at least until the moment you find yourself standing there with the hot lights blaring down on you, and thousands of eyes watching. Then reality hits you so hard that you can hardly breathe. This loss of oxygen causes that great perpetual light of understanding to go on in your head as you realize...that this was not the brightest idea you ever had.

However, I am learning.

Other people? I have my doubts sometimes. Take the two men who went hiking at a park I will leave otherwise unnamed. For political reasons of course, which is why...okay, the truth is...I can't remember my own name most of the time, much less the name of some obscure park. Unfortunately my memory happens to be one of those things that seem to be disappearing in my life. Oh, yeah, back to the story. These two men were a little nervous to be in the woods in the first place. City folk. So like those people volunteering to go on stage, they found themselves in an awkward situation. Do they give in to their uncertainty, or forge ahead? They decided that since other people do it all the time, they would forge on. However, they spent most of their walk in the woods looking down at the ground.

Snakes. They weren't especially crazy about them. But to give the snakes their due, the two men had never actually met one, so they had only their preconceived ideas to go on. Which would have been fine. Except that after awhile their preconceived ideas fell on the way side. Kind of like when that magician tells the 'volunteer' on stage that he is going to make him disappear. Only the man acts so normal about the whole thing, you start to believe that people disappear all the time. And you wave back at the audience and step inside a dark box. More curious than afraid.

Well, these two men spotted a snake. And since the snake seemed relaxed, lying in the hot sun, and hardly dangerous, they inched in closer. After further inspection, one the men, stated with great conviction, it had to be a copperhead. The other shook his head, arguing, "no, it's a water moccasin". The snake, previously uninvolved began to stir. The thing that struck me as funny is that both named a snake that was on the poisonous side, but neither man backed away from the snake. Odd. And not only did they not back away, but one of the men reached down to prove his point by grabbing the snake in the middle, thereby taking a closer look.

Snakes frown on being picked up. Not really their favorite thing. So, it firmly planted it's teeth in and latched hold of the man's arm, in self-defense. No longer lulled by the manifestation of dossal safety the man reacted as most would expect him to. Panic. He was jumping about, hollering and slinging the snake to and fro through the air. This of course only making the snake hang on tighter, which I am pretty sure, was not the man's intention.

The whole time he was battling the snake his friend was chasing him about in indecision, before finally deciding to yank the snake from his friends arm. The snake was not exactly in the best of moods by then and struck out at the rescuer. The snake was a pretty good aim as snakes go. Now they had another problem. The snake was latched onto the friends arm. Not a vast improvement to say the least.

Yet, the two friends did finally manage to dislodge the dizzy snake and make it back to civilization, via rescue one helicopter, yea it was a moccasin, and moccasins are poisonous.

Yep, just like a magic trick. There are some risks involved.

Speaking of disappearing tricks. Our lake is doing one. It is a little spooky. For instance I never knew there were all those trees and stumps out in the lake. Not to mention fishhooks and trotlines lying in wait for the unsuspecting swimmer. Ken asked if I wanted to go knee boarding and the first thing I said was..."Are you insane?! There are about a thousand things that could kill me out there." He calmly replied that it should be safer because at least I can 'see' them now. Somehow that comforts me not in the least. I could probably 'see' the saw the magician was using to cut me in half with but that would hardly be a comfort. Needless to say...I didn't go.

Speaking of pulling a rabbit out of a hat. A park visitor threw a fit in the office the other day. Seems our maps of the lake are all wrong. When our ranger asked what exactly was wrong with them, she replied, "The Lake is a lot smaller than this and there are all sorts of unmarked points the map fails to show." A grin tugged at the park ranger's mouth, before he reminded her that the lake was a little different than when the map was made. A summer of drought and being over nine feet low will do that to near anything with water in it. She blushed.

I suppose the only help would be to get us one of those magic type maps that change with the water level. And barring that how about a nice thick rain cloud that doesn't slide right past us.

It's All a Matter of Perspective

Did you ever notice that when asked, no two people ever come up with the same exact story, even if they were both there? Hmm…interesting. And if you were to ask further you would only become more confused. One would swear it was the worst tragedy ever imagined. The other? Well, can I help it if I find most things funny? It's in my nature.

Take the other day…when I nearly died.

And no, that is not the funny part. See, Ken and I were Kayaking on the lazy Illinois River in Oklahoma. Nice and relaxing. Gentle ripples lulling us into a false sense of security as an eagle soared overhead and scores of small fish frolicked about our boats. It was the ideal vacation. Well, at least it was before I noticed Ken acting strangely just ahead of me. He began battling the small rapids ahead as if they were a massive class four instead of the class two they resembled. I gripped my oar a little tighter.

If life has taught me one thing it's this, Ken doesn't panic unless there is a good reason to panic.

Turns out he was right. Too late, I felt a strong current yank me towards a large pile of wood blocking part of the river. All at once I found myself surrounded by rushing water and saddled up to a hodge podge of debris. Water was being sucked underneath my boat, as I paddled hard backwards, to no avail. (In case your wondering…this is still not the funny part either, but it is exciting huh?) Anyway, I couldn't get out. Water was too deep. Dirt embankment? Too high and too steep. And I couldn't paddle out. Trouble.

Suddenly I heard Ken's soothing voice from the other side of the river. My heart instantly relaxed a bit. He would save me. Only he didn't. A puzzled frown wrinkled up my forehead. Something was definitely wrong here. Instead of comforting me, he was actually shouting at me. My frown deepened, the swirling waters no longer having my full attention. Then to my complete astonishment I realized exactly what the love of my life was saying to me. Not, "Hang in there Darling." Oh no, the man was actually saying inane things like, "Get out of there." And, "why did you go over there in the first place."

Glaring back, I shouted, "Now why didn't I think of that, and I was having such a good time too." Meanwhile my boat continued to play teeter-totter on top of the small surge of water I was stuck on. But one thing had changed. I was no longer scared. I was furious.

When informed of the fact, Ken actually had the audacity to…smile. Then very deliberately he said, "Good. Now pull yourself back on those roots hanging off the embankment and get out of there." Oh, I was getting out of there all right and then I was going to push him and his kayak right back into that cold relentless water. Besides, shouldn't he be giving me a little sympathy right now? Or at the very least be forging the river and sacrificing his life or something?

"Well, what are you waiting for? Get going."

So much for the hero who dies for his mate. At this point it hardly mattered that I knew logically that if he tried to save me his kayak would have rammed me into the pile and thrown me to my death. Or even that he would have drowned before ever reaching me. All that was beside the point.

Worked up to a good mad now, I started pulling myself back, mumbling under my breath. The whole time Ken kept shouting encouragements (I guess that is what you call them) at me. And I? Well, I no longer cared about the water trying to suck me under, I was going to get out of that dang water and throttle Ken. With that one thought guiding me, it took exactly four tries and two very sore arms later, but I did it.

And when I got out of the boat, furious as all get out?

Ken winked. Then said much too caviler, "Your welcome. I knew you could do it. You just needed to get mad."

It always does ruin a good mad when someone is laughing at you.

The other day I was in Wills Point and this nice woman was telling me about raising her two sons and how ornery they both were. She said they were always wrestling and carrying on something fierce. Until one day, as she busied herself inside, she heard this terrible crashing sound and came running. Once she reached the back, she stopped dead in her tracks. There before her lay a bucket that had been thrown clean through the back window. She was not pleased, to put it mildly. No, furious would probably better describe it. Storming into the yard, she began shouting at the offender. Now how, you may ask, did she know which one did it? Oh, the guilty ones are always easy to recognize. They are the ones standing stock still, with wide eyes and shaking head. One hand held up to ward off evil. Which would be you.

As she zeroed in on the guilty party, he quickly explained.

"Mom, it's not my fault – Kevin ducked."

Ahh…see it's all a matter of perspective.

The Scam Artist

Our park has all sorts of visitors. Most of them are good honest folk. But ever once in a while we have a different sort that come out here. And they are...well...let's just say, 'not exactly the trust worthy sort'. Which creates a little drama in our otherwise fairly mundane existence.

Take the couple in a run down van that decided to park right across from the office. It had been one of those days. Ken was running from one small park emergency to another and for a fairly long time he simply didn't have time to deal with them. But every few minutes another park host or a ranger would find and inform Ken of the uninvited visitors who refused to leave the park.

When asked to either pay or leave, they said it was near impossible seeing as they didn't have any gas. So, one park ranger asked if he could call someone. They didn't know a soul. Hmmm...

To top it off, the man swore his wife (who threw a hand to her forehead and fell into a chair as Ken approached) had MS. Most everyone in the office rolled their eyes, but hey, I thought they should get some sort of drama award. Not everyone can cover both bases of, a stranger without a friend, and a sad disability in one fatal swoop.

Anyway, Ken finally got a moment and went over to talk with them. The whole way over he was bombarded with tales of woe being told him by the other employees. He simply held up one hand and smiled, stating once more, "I'll handle it."

And when he got there? He cleared his throat, put his thumbs in his gun belt and asked three simple questions:

"What is wrong?"

The woman clutched the chair and pretended to be on the verge of fainting. The man shook his head slowly, "Out of gas".

Ken nodded, sympathic like (sort of) "Is there anyone we could call for you?"

The man looked sadly away (Probably because Ken was studying him so intensely) "Don't know anybody around these parts."

To which Ken shrugged and said, "Well, I guess I will just have to call the wrecker to pick your van up and you can ride into town with him. Do you have a preference to which one I call?"

The man's wide-eyed look of shock was his only answer. The woman, who suddenly developed unknown powers of strength, sprang to her feet. Her rounded eyes cutting fearfully over to the man.

Ken pretended he didn't notice them sprinting for the door. He did, however, hear the squeal of tires as they jumped into their van and sped away.

I guess they had enough gas after all.

I think a lot of life is like that. You sometimes can't take things at face value. You have to delve deeper to get the true story. And this is true even with the good things of life.

Take weddings for instance. By the time your sitting out in an audience it looks all snazzy and put together but…if you look closer?

Mikea got married this weekend and it went off without a hitch. Well, that is, except for one little problem. See, Mikea is short. And we never had the opportunity to have her petticoat and her gown together in the same city at the same time until the night before the wedding. And one look at the two of them together told us, that unless she borrowed a pair of stilts, she could pretty much count on her deceptively gorgeous gown dragging on the ground and tripping her up. Either on the way down the aisle or in a headfirst tumble down the steep steps of the church. Not exactly the way she wanted to be remembered on her wedding day.

Not to worry.

We got a hoola hoop. Yep, a nice sparkly blue one. And we pinned it to the bottom of her petticoat. Problem solved. Well, at least until she attempted to sit down. Opps.

Still, she looked beautiful in her elegant wedding gown sailing gracefully down the aisle. The soft sound of swishing beads inside the hoola hoop adding to the moment...and producing a small secretive smile to my daughter's face.

It was completely perfect. Or so it seemed.

Stick

I saw a friend of mine on the news a couple of months ago. His name was 'Stick'. And I was both surprised and delighted. Because you see he was one of my inspirations. One of those nice surprises that comes in weird packaging. Let me explain.

A few (okay, maybe longer than a few) years ago I lived in a small town called Bluff Dale. Now I am still not sure why they called it this, for you had to drive a bit to even come across anything that even closely resembled a bluff. Personally I think some of our ancestors just named these towns wistfully. For instance have you ever been to Colorado Springs? Don't unless you're prepared for a dust storm. How about Sweetwater? It's known for rattlesnakes. And then you have the city of Big Springs…which I am hard pressed to even find a spring. Funny.

Anyway, back to my point. I am bad a chasing rabbit trails. I went there, to Stick's house, as a favor for someone else. So, dragging my three little ones with me, I hurried over to do my good deed for the day and get back to more important tasks. But something strange happened when I walked through that door. Time slowed down a bit. He had the nicest smile. And he was funny. Both which took me by surprise. See, Stick was a paraplegic. Had been since an accident on the football field when he was in high school. When I visited him he was in his early sixties (or there about), and you would think after lying in a bed most of his life he would have been just a little bitter. He wasn't. Quite the opposite. He told me how lucky he was; I must have raised an eyebrow at him, for he quickly explained. "Had the best parents a boy could wish for, and have gotten to meet some of the nicest people." I was hooked.

After that I would stop by every once in awhile just to talk. He cheered me up. I asked him how he got the name Stick. I expected some great story. It wasn't. He said his uncle saw him playing in mud with a stick and started calling him that and it...stuck. Sorry, couldn't resist. Then he preceded to tell me about going fishing during the depression with a telephone. Hmmm. I heard of calling up a deer, but a fish? I'm a little puny today. Sorry, I'll stop now.

Seems they would wind up one of those old fashion kind of phones until they would create a bit of an electric shock, then they would shock the Carp and scoop them right up. I was fascinated. It seemed a little ingenious to me, but personally I think dynamite would have been a little less trouble. He was full of stories, even when he died. Which is why he made the Dallas News. He touched others even from a bed.

I wonder if most people even realize when their impressing folks.

Take the Squirrel Lady. A friend of mine said she was once helping someone plan a wedding in Arkansas. They had picked the prettiest flowers. The perfect place. The gown. Now all they needed was a cake. So, on hearing about this one dear lady, they went out to her place to have a talk with her. Which apparently was their first mistake.

They no sooner got started then her shirt started dancing about. Which was a little distracting to say the least. My friend cut her eyes over at the young bride, who had a shocked look on her face. They weren't sure if they were in an alien movie or the blockbuster Deliverance, but either one was not a pleasant thought. So they tried to act as if nothing was the matter. Even when a squirrel popped his furry head out at them from the collar of her shirt. They might have yelped, but the lady kept on discussing cakes as if nothing out of the ordinary was going on. And I've no doubt for her there wasn't.

Did she make the cake? Nope. But my friend and the bride waited to tell her over the phone. I don't think they knew exactly what to say at the time. And to be honest probably didn't have enough dealings with Squirrel people to know how to respond. So they didn't. Probably a wise move.

But regardless, she made quite an impression.

Motorcycle people out here at the park impress me. Last month we had a whole slew of folks come out with some pretty snazzy wheels. Little pop up trailers, shiny helmets, and leather jackets. I get a little envious every time I see them come out here camping together. Oh, to be free. The open road. Wind tugging at your hair as you going flying down a smooth pavement. But alas, such freedom is never to be mine.

See, I have this leaning problem. Every time I reach a curve...I freeze. Then in a blind panic I react by leaning the opposite way of the curve. Not a good thing. Especially if you're the one driving. I gather it is a little unnerving by the sound of Ken's voice roaring, "Lean Tammy, Lean!" Which only makes me lean harder - in the wrong direction. Trouble.

But the other day I saw this motorcycle that I think I could ride. It was cool. It had a front seat and a double back seat, with shiny metal pipes coming back over their heads like something out of the 'Munsters'. Cool. But most of all it had three, count them, three wheels. I think I could manage to not kill us with three wheels. What do you think?

Yeah. Me too. Impressed or not, I better stick with four.

Have a wonderful Christmas and make sure and leave an impression...the good kind.

Tempting Fate

Have you ever tempted fate? The whole time you know the odds are against you, but for some insane reason you just can't seem to stop yourself. It is rather like that silly moth in "A bug's life". He is heading for disaster in the form of a bug zapper, while the whole time telling his friend, "I can't stop...it's so beautiful." Well, the other morning a man from Dallas found himself in the same predicament. Only it wasn't a bug zapper, but our lake calling out through a dense fog to him.

After traveling all the way from Dallas, no doubt picturing a peaceful day floating along our lake and leisurely pulling up catfish from their watery home, he arrived only to find the entire lake covered in fog. A lesser man would have given up. But being the optimistic sort, he backed his boat into the water, certain the fog would lift any moment. It didn't. Still, determined to have his day of fishing, he opened the throttle and maneuvered through our ever narrowing channel leading to the middle of the lake.

Now he had a decision to make. Did he stay happily bobbing up and down in the middle of the lake? Or instead did he gamble on his inability to decipher land from water, and head inland where he knew the catfish were waiting for him? All these thoughts likely ran through his eager mind, before he made that fatal decision. Finally, he decided to press his luck and head further inland. And all I have to say is...

He was successful. Well, at least in heading the right direction. In fact it didn't take him very long at all to find land in true James Bond fashion. Smoothly and confidently he ran that sleek boat right up on the land with hardly a bump to slow him down. When he did exit the boat, why...he didn't even get his feet wet. So, after walking completely around his buried boat, he decided this was a job bigger than one man could handle and went in search of help. Now the bad thing about running a boat aground is there isn't a whole lot of willing souls to help with a thing like that. Oh, there were jokes thrown his direction, shaking of heads and outright laughter, but not a lot of help. All day, as he and his brothers dug out that boat, spectators would come by and just watch in awe. After all, they had never seen a boat buried in the mud, much less one having to be dug out. Of course they didn't offer help, only stated how they would never drive a boat up on land in a fog. I, myself wouldn't have said such a thing. Everyone knows if you say 'never', then you just tempted fate. Oh, well, more boats to rescue.

Anyway, the project of boat excavation took two full days. Finally it was ready to be pulled out by his two brothers (the only people who have to help you out of jam) each waiting in eager expectation from their own boats. Ken and Beth (our Office Manager) came along just in time to help. An hour later Ken came home for supplies and me, and we set out to conquer the boat. It was fun. There is something confidence building about rocking a boat loose and shoving it into the water. They should offer classes. How to feel like a superhero in ten easy rocks. Or better yet, how about a new sort of exercise routine to help get you into shape. We could offer to run a boat up on land every couple of days and people could pay us to have the opportunity to enrich their lives. Hey, I've seen stranger things, why not boat excavation?

Well, this must be the time of year for tempting fate, because the other night Ken got a call to rescue three men adrift in their boat. Again people scoffed at the silliness of grown men. Imagine? Not bringing paddles in case your motor fails. But when Ken eased up on the men, they were plain tuckered out. Seems they had paddles. But to tell you the truth, one was 82, one 79 and the youngest, who was 59 had a slight disadvantage. He had only one arm. I don't know about you, but I think it wouldn't have mattered how many paddles they had. Regardless, they had defied the taunting voice of reason and took their chances on that dark night.

And Ken took their boat and towed them home.

My sister likes to tempt fate as well. See, we carry a similar family trait. We set booby traps. Oh, not the kind that catch criminals or lions, but the kind that make you hurt yourself trying get out of the way of falling objects. Never mind that we have precariously placed the said objects ourselves. Ken hates this game, but that's another story. Anyway, we are usually wise enough to not get caught in our own traps but one day that elusive, "I can defeat the odds", slipped over my sister's common sense and lured her into her own demise.

She was making potato soup. In fact, she was starving for it. Dreaming of its creamy essence all day, so that once she started making it she was hurrying about, mouth watering in expectation. Hands flew as she chopped and diced her way to satisfaction. Then suddenly she stopped. Was it three or five cups of milk? She glanced up at the cabinet over the stove, and frowned. For she knew she had stuffed many a recipe into it's depths with not a thought of future retrieval. She also knew that they were stacked hodgepodge over her head...waiting. Now she knew the odds were not in her favor to pull those recipes out and not have at least some fall out on her head, but the soup was calling her name, insisting she take the chance. So, very carefully, she reached up and securely clamped the loose pieces of paper together and pulled them out of the trap. And she would have succeeded too, if it hadn't had been for the candles.

Apparently some other family member, also with the inherited booby trap gene, had shoved a handful of candles on top of the papers before slamming the door shut and waiting for their next victim. As candles bombarded my sister's head, the papers went flying, and in her valiant attempt to catch some of the articles bombarding her body, she knocked over her coke which flung itself throughout the kitchen, emptying out as it went. Then as she clung to a few recipes shoved up against the air vent, she heard it. The dreaded plop. Looking down she saw one flower candle, floating serenely for half a second before being submerged into her precious soup.

It was not a pretty picture.

So, I guess if we are to learn anything from tempting fate, it is;

- Boats and fogs don't make good companions
- Three men and a paddle are usually in need of a rescue
- And finally, you can't have your candles and eat them too

Have a wonderful Thanksgiving!

The Bad Name Bunny

Did you ever notice that there are some awfully strange occurrences that come from combining two unlikely variables? In other words…some things just don't have any business associating with each other…it's just weird.

Take bunnies. If in the country they live in nice rabbit holes. Doing rabbit things. We take pictures of them. Sneak up on them in awe, holding out a trembling hand with some offering of food. Doing so, we have experienced wildlife in its truest form.

Then there is the city rabbit. He is immaculately white and dwells in cages. We ignore him pretty much unless we are heading out the door. Then we shout over one shoulder, "Would somebody please feed that dang rabbit." And a small part of us counts down his life expectancy with eager anticipation.

Either one of these situations are normal. We understand them. However my sister experienced a different sort of rabbit. At one time he too lived in a wire cage at someone's home. Mostly ignored and well feed. But then something out of the ordinary happened. He escaped. Only being as he was tame, decided to just adopt the whole city block instead of one family. At first, filled with wonder, the town folk were entranced with his friendliness. They fed him carrots. Petted him. Let their children bond.

Until a week past. Now he began acting like a regular rabbit. He started eating all the nice potted plants. Which did not endear him to the owners. He then began chewing on anything that even vastly resembled food. Nothing was sacred. And the parents were at a dilemma. They couldn't, to the horror of their children, get rid of the rabbit. And they couldn't, to the horror of themselves, catch the silly thing. And so he happily continued munching away on their well-manicured gardens, earning the title, "the bad name bunny".

See, some things are just wrong.

Take camping. I have seen some things that make me pause and say, "Something is wrong with this picture." But only time eventually reveals it to me. For instance we had a man who came camping for the first time with a boy scouts troop. He pulled up in his hummer and asked a bunch of questions about how to set up camp. Then zipping into a spot, amid confused stares, proceeded to pull out his little dinky tent and sleeping bags. See? Wrong. Hummers and dinky tents just don't go together.

I've seen chandelier lights over a picnic table. Old sputtering trucks pulling brand spanking new fishing boats. And vehicles that take off on the 'hiking' trail. I have even seen dogs strapped to their owner's chest… bouncing along trails and zipping around on bikes. This too is wrong. Dogs belong on the ground. Running happily through the woods and becoming hopelessly lost, or nipping joyfully at bike tires. This is normal. This I can understand. Owners carrying a dog on a hike? Well, this is a little confusing to me.

Yet, I must be a little odd myself. For to tell you the truth, these people and my sister's no name bunny, are the highlights of my day. They just make life more interesting.

Who knows? Maybe I should try something out of the ordinary. Do you think they make a backpack big enough for a Weimaraner?

The Bluebird Of Happiness And Other Myths

Did you know a bluebird is actually not blue at all?

It isn't. The bluebird's wings somehow reflect and absorb different parts of the light creating the seemingly blue color. In other words, the color you see? Well, it is all in the eye of the beholder. Like most things in life.

Our little state park has been open a year now. And throughout this past year I have noticed the way I see the park is vastly different from the way someone else may view it. It is my home.

It is the visitor's vacation spot. The long winding trails and hidden pond are as familiar to me as your backyard. Unfortunately, some of you get a little lost in my backyard.

Some families come to see us, sit around a warm campfire, laugh and have the best time just being together. So much so, that when they come back they insist on staying in the very same spot.

As if that is the only place to capture the laughter and memories of the time before. Others come notice the ivy is poisonous, the trails muddy and beach sandy. They trade spots often trying to find that elusive perfect spot. But believe me, it is non-existent. The campsites are just campsites. You bring your view of life with you. Good or Bad.

President Lincoln said, "Most folks are as happy as they make up their minds to be." This is true. Life is full of good and bad, it is just a matter of what you decide to focus on. Take what happened to one of our park hosts, it is probably not a good idea to mention names so…we will call her … 'Caroline'.

When they moved here everything was so interesting to them- the wildlife, the birds, and the huge lake that was brimming with catfish. They were in heaven. They got so use to being awed and wowed, that they just started investing their own exciting discoveries. First, there were the battling hummingbirds.

Friends had come down to visit them and the hummingbirds were flying around – well, being hummingbirds. Suddenly, two caught their eye. They were lost in what appeared to be a fierce battle. The hummingbirds continued fighting all the way to the ground, tumbling and twirling.

The park hosts leaned in closer, beckoning their friends in close to watch the two birds frantically entwined in a battle like none they had ever seen before. Their friends kept repeating, "We don't see any hummingbirds." And the park hosts kept pointing to the two twirling figures, on the ground now.

It was then that they noticed something extremely strange had happened. The two hummingbirds had turned into twirling leaves instead. Pretty good trick huh? But, I have to ask, who was having the better time? The park hosts, or their friends?

They also discovered a screech owl living in a wood duck box. Well, actually it was the south end of a wood duck mama. But, she sure made a good screech owl, especially if you have a little imagination. And I think I mentioned the eagle that lives out here?

Well, there has been quite a lot of sighting since then. Of course, many of them have been of vultures pretending to be an eagle. Then there was the sighting of a juvenile eagle…no, make that a deformed hawk…or maybe just some weird albino eagle.

The people could never quite make up their mind for sure. Thankfully, the Osprey himself had no trouble knowing what he was.

Ken tries to explain to people, but if they insist, he just walks away smiling. After all, who is he to argue with the beholder?

Ken just came in fishless.

Seems as if a park ranger from another state park told him to hurry on over, the fish were back up in the creek and so plentiful that a man was seen dragging a huge catch up the bank behind him (Talipeia). Ken put on his Camo, fetched his bow and hightailed it over there. It was not a good sign when he got there and the other park rangers were laughing at him.

Turns out it was a little more of the beholder stuff. He failed to notice the man's wife trailing along behind the man dragging what turned out to be an empty stringer of fish, fussing about not getting one single fish all day long. But, hey…Ken needed a day away anyway. Right?

So, if you've never been to our park come on over. But be sure and bring your imagination with you, you'll have a much better time. And who knows, you might be one of the lucky ones to witness bluebirds in flight or a hummingbird fight. Beauty really is in the eye of the beholder.

The Circus Cemetery

Life is full of oddities.

At least in Hugo Oklahoma. That is where Ken and I decided to check out this deer lease and in the process found a 'circus cemetery'. That such a thing exists at all is odd in of itself, but why Oklahoma? So, I decided to check it out. After all, you can only walk around land so long before you need a diversion of sorts. And one of mine happens to be cemeteries.

So, with Ken shaking his head at me, we set off to see what a circus cemetery looked like, exactly. I couldn't even imagine, except a nice local woman said it was easy to spot their section. Hmmm. And turns out...she was right.

The first thing that catches your eye is this massive stone. I'm talking huge here. With an etched ringmaster calling you forward. It made me smile. Then scattered about are these small columns with elephants propped up on top. Not your average type cemetery plots to say the least. There were small pictures of people with their elephants, apes, horses, ect... Headstones with musical instruments, saying and even one headstone, which was a small model of a tent itself. Then there was the one that told the story of how a man died in a swimming accident while doing an act. But the nicest, and eeriest of all, was this gray marble bench under a small oak tree in memory of one of the performers. It read, 'come have a seat and I will tell you a story'. Let me tell you, I was a little nervous about that one.

But I think what caught my eye the most was all the couples buried there. The lifetimes spent in the circus. The pride in their work. The work of making people smile. Apparently, even in death. I have to admit that is not the way I pictured a circus person's life. I thought they must be miserable. Traveling around from one city to the next. No family. No friends.

Unappreciated. But going to Hugo, I realized that is not the way it is at all. From what I read, the circus itself if full of friends and families. Only they get to take them along wherever they go. Nice. Imagine, nearly every single day they get to make people, strangers, smile. Make them forget their worries if only for a couple of hours. What a wonderful way to make a living.

Oh, and the plots themselves? Donated by one of the elephant trainers so all circus people will have a place to rest. In fact, that is what it is called, the 'Showman's Rest'. I guess you can learn something new. Even in a circus cemetery.

Ken learned something new too the other night.

He came upon a lone man madly waving about a flashlight and talking frantically into a walkie-talkie. Thinking the man needed help. Whether physically or mentally, he wasn't sure, Ken pulled up and got out to help.

Turns out the man's friends, a young marine and two young women, were lost on the lake. And he kept losing contact with them. Dang walkie-talkie. Being the practical sort and watching a boat frantically darting back and forth across the lake in the distance, Ken asked if he had tried his cell phone.

The man blushed. As a matter of fact, he hadn't.

Rather sheepishly, he pulled one out and started talking to the young people who were by now over by the pump station. And out of gas. Oh, and now their cell phone was cutting out. Trouble. Now what?

Well, Ken decided to go and get his boat to help them, only when he turned to go he noticed something strange. The dead in the water boat was moving. Slowly yes, but definitely moving toward a shallow point jutting out into the water. How were they doing it? The man said there were no paddles on board yet Ken could definitely make out, as he pulled out his binoculars, one prone figure stretched out flat at the front of the boat paddling away furiously. Strange.

Soon, the two girls were let out and the young man drew ever closer to Ken and his friend. His massive strokes strong and sure. Fascinated, Ken waited. Sure enough the marine came paddling up to the boat dock sweat dripping off his flushed face. His muscles so cramped up by now that he had trouble letting go of the broom. Yes, broom. Turns out his paddle, was an old broken broom. Ken was impressed. And dying laughing. After all, it is not the average man who can paddle a boat with a broom. Funny.

As I said, life is full of oddities.

Today Ken came in for lunch a little late. Ruby and Joe, who live near here, were telling him a story. Apparently one of the youth camps in Raines County is harboring some teenage boys from New Orleans that were in Detention centers. City kids. They were a little worried about them taking off. But they needn't have been.

Seems city kids are a little leery of East Texas. And especially living out in the country. Just the other evening, a whole herd of them came flying back into the building, talking excitedly and breathing heavily. They saw something outside. It was horrible. So horrible in fact that they would never go outside again.

When questioned further, they finally were able to get out what had frightened them so bad. It was a baby dinosaur! And they had seen enough movies to know that the mama dinosaur had to not be far behind. Floored, one of the counselors looked outside to see this strange creature that had run off hardened city kids.

It was an armadillo. Which I guess looks sort of like a dinosaur. At least if you're from New Orleans it must.

See, oddities.

I think the bottom line is that we live in a strange world sometimes. And truth be told, I rather think God made it that way on purpose. As the clown prayer says (I read it at Angie's Circus Diner), "the clown only hopes he can make people smile in this crazy life, and in the process, he hopes God smiles a little too." What could be nicer than that?

The Gathering

Did you ever notice there are some awfully odd gatherings in this old world? Well, I just experienced one recently on my yearly trip to Kansas to visit my sister. It's called the "STAG".

I don't know how the thing got started, and I'm not even sure they do, but it goes something like this...

Masses of men (we are talking well over 300) from all over the country gather in this small Kansas town. I use the term 'town' lightly. I think it has one store, one school, one post office, one gas station and one church. Anyway, the night before pheasant season starts people (men) gather at the 'hall' and play poker till the early hours of the morning and eat fried chicken and sheep 'fries'. I believe we have the eqivalent here called calf 'fries'. Weird. Anyway, all the men claim to like the things, especially the young boys. Personally I think it must be some sort of rite of passage to manhood and pheasant hunting because you can't convince me they are really any good. I mean seriously, who in the world would actually think, "you know seems a waste so I believe I'll just eat that tongue, brains, 'fries' and see if it kills me or not." All I can say is I would have to be pretty desperate and pretty hungry to even think of such a thing. Personally, I think the whole tradition must have started on a dare and then it became a matter of pride. Now no one would dare own up to disliking the things. Yep, I bet their ancestors are dying laughing right now.

Anyway, the next morning, these same bleary-eyed men put on bright orange vests and gather up guns. Traipse through stubble fields and shoot pheasants from the air. I am told this is a very enjoyable experience, if you're the pheasant hunting sort. However, the guides tell a different story. See, there are these "New Yorkers", as they are called who fly in every year to participate in this ritual. Unfortunately they know very little about Kansas's farmers and even less about pheasant hunting. Trouble.

Come morning these men are geared up for an adventure of a lifetime. Not one actually owns his own shotgun of course. So after a quick lesson, they start walking. Excitement making them jumpy and their trigger finger itch. Before long the planted pheasants break out in front of them the sun glinting off their colorful feathers. And then what happens? Shotguns point haphazardly in the air and at those around them before going off at will. And if any pheasants happen to actually die during this process? Well, I am pretty sure it is just an accident. And why you may ask would a clear-headed Kansas farmer subject himself to such a punishment year after year? To nearly die at a strange New Yorker's hand in this yearly game of dodge the bullet? When asked they simply say, "They sure do tip well."

Call me strange but I don't believe they tip that well.

The last couple of months have been a time for gathering up different sort of people. We have had two hurricanes. Which the State Park was one of the places refugees could go. We didn't get any from Louisiana, but we did from Rita. That was a crazy moment, wasn't it? We had some very nice and extremely patient people pull in the night before the hurricane hit. Some of them had been on the road for over twelve hours. One group of refugees came in four cars, had two tents and seven, I repeat seven, dogs. Whew. I would have hated to make that trip. If it had been me, some people or dogs would have had to go. And depending on the people, the dogs might have won out.

I don't know about you but it sure has been a strange year. And even a stranger one for 'gatherings'. Thank goodness it is finally over and Thanksgiving is right around the corner. I don't know about you but the whole thing makes me a little nervous. It sounds good in theory. Gather your entire family around a huge table, all in one house, stuff them full of sacrificial turkey, and then just sit back for some good conversation. But it hardly ever goes that smooth for me.

For one thing I tend to cram too many things in. While most people are watching football, I drag my family out to play it. Which would not be a bad thing if the majority of them weren't girls. My sister (the model girl) is usually drug out on the field snarling under her breath, "I absolutely hate football." Then there are the boys who role their eyes at having to repeat for the fifteenth time what a 'down' is, and why the girls can't have one.

Needless to say, by the time it's all said and done, I walk off feeling fairly pleased with myself for helping 'bond' the family. My sister on the other hand leaves limping and groaning about a broke nail. While my girls, now that the torture has ended, are finally laughing at the ridiculous experience and the boys end up tossing the football all the way home. In fact, the only real throwing they get to do all day. And why do I subject my family to this torture?

Well now that you mention it I'm not exactly…hey, wait a minute…isn't Thanksgiving a gathering? Trouble.

<u>The One That Got Away</u>

Now you know I'm not one to complain about my husband.

Okay. Maybe I do complain a little. Still, this time I swear you will be on my side when I tell you what happened. Especially since you will never actually get to hear his side. It's one of the advantages of writing in a newspaper. Getting the last word.

Anyway, it all started with a seemingly nice invitation from one of our park hosts. He said to call him 'Curtis'. Of course his name is Jimmy, but I won't tell if you don't. He invited Ken and I to go fishing with him on his boat. Together. The both of us. You see why I say it was a 'seemingly' nice invitation. The man has been married a long time and you can't tell me he didn't know what he was doing.

He peacefully backed the boat into the water and announced we were going jig fishing. How excited I was. The sun bouncing off the water. The morning air holding it's promise of a boat load of fish. Ahhh. Perfection.

There was just one little problem. I had never been jig fishing. And personally I think some amateur fisherman like myself got bored one day and made it up. No doubt he started dipping his line up and down in the water unknowingly bothering the aggravated fish below until finally...and I'm sure, accidentally...a most irritated fish charged at the offending lure. Low and behold, jig fishing was born.

To tell the truth, I'm not very good at it. You have to 'jig' it just right. This means...well, I'm not sure exactly what it means...I just know that like that first fisherman, the few I got were just plain luck.

But, I tried to act like I knew what I was doing. This is extremely important when you are doing anything with your husband. Otherwise, he will take it upon himself to help you. This is rarely a good thing.

After a lengthy period of watching my inefficiency, Ken could stand it no more and started helping. He told me where to put my line. How deep to drop it. And how to hold the pole. About the only thing he didn't do was take over the fishing himself.

After a few deadly glares his direction, he shrugged and let me fish on my own. Deciding no doubt, that one more helpful hint might have landed him in the lake with a little help from me. Girls rarely like to be told what to do. We can mess up all by ourselves, thank you.

Besides, after awhile I did start catching fish.

Not many of them were Crappie, but hey - they were fish. Let's see. I caught perch, a bass, a few crappie and then...oh, yes...a catfish.

And we are not talking a small insignificant catfish. It must have weighed 100 pounds! Okay, maybe more like fifteen. But, it was huge to me. I was bouncing up and down in the boat. Both excited and deathly afraid I would lose the battle waging between me and my Moby Dick.

I kept shouting for Ken to do something. He just raised an eyebrow and grinned. Perhaps I shouldn't have declined his help earlier. Now I was on my own. But, I was determined.

For several minutes I fought. Biting my tongue in concentration. Muscles bulging under the strain. Probably because they were not use to so much effort on my part. Whatever the reason, soon all discomforts faded away.

I took no notice of the blazing sun. Or the sweat gathering under my eyes. Even the fact that the two men in the boat with me were catching Crappie left and right was lost on me. Nothing else existed besides that monster below and me.

And then he surfaced. He was mine. All mine. Ken reached down and pulled him up, a look of distaste on his face. "It's a yellow cat."

Everything happened so fast. One moment it was there and then...gone. I couldn't believe it. After all that effort. Who cares I was not the one to clean it. Who cares I don't even like eating yellow cats either. That is beside the point. I captured it. I deserved to bask in the glory.

Or not.

Oddly enough Jimmy still asks us to go fishing. Together. Personally, I think it's for the entertainment. His.

TO OUR READERS: *Mrs. Watson is not aware that when she asked her husband to e-mail her Life In The Park column, that he attached his side of the story.*

Despite the alleged assistance I gave my wife through the duration of the fishin' trip, I thought y'all might like to know, as Paul Harvey would say, "the rest of the story". Besides, I've heard it said many times over the last two years that I should defend myself more vigorously, prior to publication.

First of all, and for the record, "jig" fishin' ain't got a thing to do with bouncin' yer bottom, kickin' up your heals, or any other gyration of the anatomy, particularly while your in the boat flailing' a fishin' pole around your head.

Now as to the "help", (which was merely advice based upon personal experience), once Tammy knew how to operate the jig in the proper manner, she caught most of the fish, true they was mostly short ones or the wrong species, but...still when she set the hook on that "Moby Dick" fish, it was on.

Why, I think we could have sold tickets to the show, graduate level instructions on "JIG" fishin', her hollerin' for help must have attracted half the boats on the lake to the rescue, it was better than TV, most entertaining.

Now let me just clarify, that when one gets an invite to go Crappie fishin', one should expect to catch Crappie, not every other species of aquatic life in the lake.

With that said, who wants a fifteen-pound Catfish in the livewell with all those Crappies? So yes, I did let the fish go....you should'a-seen the look on her face, guess that'll teach her.

Wasn't long then before she smacked me in the face from behind with her rod tip, said she was settin' the hook on a Crappie but....I guess it got away.

The Trouble With Critters

I know it's not politically correct, but…well, I'm going to kill this dang dog.

We're going through this transitional state. Mine, not hers. Give her a couple of more weeks and she should just about have me broken in.

Yes, the trouble all started about 40 something years ago. The day I was born. From then on we have celebrated these things called birthdays where we envision the perfect day. Presents piled up, laughing friends…ahhh, the shear magic of it all.

Which is why I asked for a dog. Of course, what I really wanted was the illusion of a dog. Not a real dog. That kind that chews up things and smells funny. No, I wanted the kind of dog you see in "Old Yeller."

Coat shiny and tangle free. Faithful, calm and clean. The kind that would die for you and hang on your every word. I envisioned long walks with her close to my side. A silent companion, well mannered and easy to live with. Yes, a nice little addition to our family. And in that respect, I guess I was right.

We got a new baby. A 40-pound baby, that is.

I find her cuddled up on my furniture and I drag her off. Sitting down for me is impossible now. If I do a giant dog leaps up and lands hard on my middle.

Even my family is not amused. Mikea kept looking longingly at the sofa the other night while trying to eat a burrito standing up. "I just want to be able to sit down for one minute without her on top of me." Such a dreamer she is.

Ken fluctuates between shouting and petting. She is, after all – my "gift." He is trying to be nice. Which is not easy considering everyone in the whole house is sleep deprived.

She cries half the night and wakes me at five to go out. Which wouldn't be bad if she didn't whine to come back in and then whine when I put her back up.

My sweet easygoing daughter is getting just a wee bit cranky to say the least. She now glares at all of us, and swears off her ever having children. Promising a return of my former child if I think of some way she can just get some sleep.

I think everyone goes through this, in one form or another. We never really believe some animal can get grown people mad enough to spit and shout, while stomping all over our favorite hat. But, they can.

I remember my brother-in-law who lives on a farm up in Kansas. How he would look at me when he still lived in the city and say how perfect everything would be if he could just get up to the farm.

I don't think he's had a full night's sleep since he got there. See, a farm has lots of critters. Pigs that chase you and forget they have little pigs, so decide to take a nap on them. Not good. Dogs that chase cows. Not always in the direction you would like. And sheep...well, we all knows how dumb sheep are.

But, I think the funniest story my sister told was when they spent all day loading up cows to take from one field to another. They were tired and not very pleasant by the end of the day. But, they managed to load the last of the cows up in the trailer.

Of course, they were barely speaking by this time. One because it would have required more energy than they possessed and two, because getting mad at cows is not nearly as productive as getting mad at each other.

As they slammed the doors shut and started the ignition, my sister ground out something about did he double check the lock on the trailer. He growled back, something about did he look like an idiot, of course he locked the trailer. Then in seething silence he put the trailer in motion, determined to get rid of the cows by dark and have some supper.

Perhaps my sister would have heard the weird sound sooner, had she not been sulled up angry.

Luckily she was looking off out the window and caught a rather strange reflection. Cows tumbling out the back of the trailer and rolling down the road like potatoes out of a tow sack. She leaned over in disbelief and couldn't decide whether to laugh or cry. Laughing won out. Let's just say it was well after dark before they got any supper.

Well, now my puppy is all peaceful and well mannered beside me. And I feel a twinge of guilt for being aggravated a moment ago. She is so sweet and innocent looking…when she's asleep.

There is Only One Way to Test That...

You can learn a lot of things from a bug man.

The last time we had our house sprayed, the bug man and Ken got to talking about hunting dogs. I guess the fact that mine were yelping about beside them might have been what got them to thinking. Whatever it was, I was glad I happened across their conversation and just sat back, soaking it all in. Okay, maybe you might call it ease dropping, but you can learn quite a bit from listening in on other's conversation.

One thing I learned was that...fathers and sons? Don't exactly communicate as well as most folks do. Maybe it is because the son has not yet fully developed the men's code way of talking. Whatever it is, unlike the women in their lives who ask a million questions, they resort to acting first and asking questions later. Which, as you can imagine, can create somewhat of a problem. Especially when it comes to shock collars.

See, most men are the curious sort. They like and use gadgets that make their lives easier. For instance, years ago no one had even heard of a shock collar. No, most men forged ahead using more primitive and time-consuming methods of training. It was a slow and tedious endeavor that work weary men have little patience for nowadays, so they use shock collars instead. Yes siree, if you want a dog to stop, that'll do it. Well, in most cases anyway. Turns out that when a stubborn dog gets use to the thing, it will hardly slow him down if the hunt is worth the pain to him. Which makes the man holding the gadget? Curious.

One exasperated man told his son, "Son, I want to test this thing out. See exactly how much of a shock that dog is getting." The son responded by nodding in that distracted teenage way. Which his dad falsely assumed was an indication that he was listening. "I'll put the thing on and stand off a bit, and then when I raise my hand you shock me." The son, who is by now probably contemplating the gadget his father just handed him, again nods. Unfortunately, what he hears is, "shock me when I raise my hand." All other words lost in translation. I am sure he might have thought this did not sound exactly right, but as his father was frustrated and bellowing, not to mention speaking in an authorative tone - the youth simply looked up and said, "Okay, dad."

Now the man plods out to the center of the field and raises his hand. To which, the obedient son presses the button. The man is shocked all right. Senseless it seems. So rather than taking the thing off he starts waving his hands in genuine panic. Again the son, smiling…shocks him…only longer this time. After all, since his dad is waving more excitedly now, it must mean that his dad wishes to be shocked longer and more intensely. This assumption is met by more mad waving, shouts and jerking at the collar, as his son…pleasantly continues shocking him. This goes on until at last, the man finally gains his senses and runs up, jerking the gadget out of his son's hands. Ranting and raving now at him, instead of the dog. Who, no doubt, is by this time chuckling at his human's lack of sanity. Even he would not put the thing on himself.

I thought this was just a one time occurrence, but it turns out that a friend of Ken's fell into the same trap. He too had a dog that when shocked would stop a minute; bear down and then continue to run. But he was a little more logical about his test. Rather than let someone else shock him. He put the thing on and - shocked himself.

After he stopped dancing about while saying some rather choice words, he took it off. And decided that from now on he would just trust that the thing was working. After all, there is only one way to test that little theory…

A couple of weeks ago a game warden nearly ran over an alligator. Knowing it was too close to the road and people's houses, he decided to relocate it. Which, if you have ever attempted taping an alligator's mouth and capturing it when it doesn't exactly like the experience well, let's just say he wasn't having the best of times.

Which only improved when a lady came driving by to offer her help - to the alligator. Now, while he was trying to wrestle the thing, she started lecturing him on the proper way to treat a poor defenseless alligator. After all, the critter should be free to wander at will, doing alligator things, not tied up and thrown into the back of a pickup. It was inhuman. The game warden, sweating and exhausted, tried to reason with her, but between the alligator not cooperating about getting in the truck and the woman berating him constantly, he decided to just get the thing in there and leave. He would tie him up better, once he was out of sight of the animal lover. The alligator, not knowing he was simply being relocated to his natural habitat, decided to jump ship. You can imagine the game warden's surprise when he looked in his rearview mirror only to see his previously captured alligator, waddling away down the road as fast as his little legs would carry him. He instantly stopped the truck and went back, wrestled the critter (tying up his legs this time) and with muscles quivering shoved him back into the bed of the truck.

What happened to the lost alligator? I am happy to report that he slid quietly in the water of his new home, no worse for wear after his grand adventure. And what would have happened if the game warden had decided to leave the alligator there in the country within walking distance of the road and people's homes. Maybe nothing. Or maybe, like when we lived in Huntsville, people's dogs would start to disappear, among other things. I don't know for sure, but one thing I do know is…well, there is only one way to test that theory and personally, after sharing a small lake with alligators in Huntsville, I'd rather they stay on their side and I'll stay on mine.

There Ought to be a Sign!

I have about decided there ought to be a sign in front of our new bicycle trail that reads, 'no one between the ages of 10 and 14 may go on this trail, unless you desire to be lost, hunted down by irate parents and finally saved by a ranger'. Of course once having been a teenager myself years ago and having raised several, I know it would be pretty much useless. Kids would take it as a challenge. It's in their makeup.

Which is why, since opening up the trail, we have had three sets of kids lost in its depths. Some not even on a bicycle. It seems to call out to them. Oddly enough little ones don't dare go down the small narrow path, and older folks seem to find their way around pretty easily...so it is just that one age group...I wonder why? But regardless of why, I do know the steps leading up to the decision.

1. First it is slightly forbidden. Trail says, bicycles only, which is a challenge in of itself.
2. It is narrow and wooded. The path less taken and all that.
3. Everyone else (common sense type) is afraid to enter it. Which makes the more adventuresome (lost type) even more excited about the whole idea. Indiana Jones type mentality.
4. And finally, it is way cool to try and get lost at this age. Why I can't say exactly except...it is.
5. They split up. The more cautious type take back the opposite direction.

Then it would be a loss of pride for the others to turn back. Even if they rethink their position on the matter. Going back would then make them, horror of horrors, chicken. Not ever a good thing at this age.

And so because of these five seductions, twice Ken and I have gone into the woods after them. Both times we met them coming out. Wide eyed, exhausted and very thirsty. One group even leaving a string of paraphilnalia scattered down the trail behind them, as they shed excess weight. Reminding me a little of past wagon train movies, throwing out their heirlooms to lighten the load. Kids make me laugh. Regardless, the good thing is…they do find their way out. And after all, it isn't a very long trail to begin with…well, at least on a bike it isn't.

I am just glad that once we get older, we outgrow all of that. Take the other day at Lake Quachita in Arkansas; I was standing there enjoying all the beauty around me. The trees, the lake…the three Sisters Spring. Reading about years ago when people use to come and drink the waters to be cured. Very interesting. In the process I looked down and noticed one of the springs was suppose to cure my aliment. Cool. So being the responsible, rational person I am, I gathered me up some in a container. After all, it is worth a try, right? I mean, what could it hurt?

Only that the water might possibly not be purified. Or be downright bad for you nowadays. But surely, if that were true, there would be a sign, right?

Oh yeah…there was one.

To Do, or Die

The other day while walking Gracie, I saw an interesting way to teach your offspring to ride a bike. It is called the 'the do, or die' theory.

It goes something like this; you take a few moments before you leave on a camping trip, stuff your big eyed little one on his new two wheeler, give him a quick lesson, then shove the two into the pickup and head out for the REAL lesson. Oh, and don't forget to bring reinforcement in the form of two big brothers.

Once setting up your camper and gathering up safety gear (you wouldn't want anyone to get hurt) you head out for the bike trial. The wobbling little one, white knuckling the handlebars for dear life and playing dodge ball with the trees, while the older two shout encouragements from up ahead such as, "Are you coming, or what?!" Yep. The do or die method. Whether he lives or not is totally up to him. Don't quote me on it, but I believe this method was also used long ago to teach some youngsters to swim. Hence the old saying, "Sink or Swim" came into being. Literally.

Although I am not sure if I recommend this technique, it does seem to prepare you for life. Sometimes the only way to learn something is to jump right in there and do it...and if you survive the experience? Well, then next time it will come a little easier. After all, I am sure that after the boy got home from camping, those straight city streets where a piece of cake compared to the tree infested bike trail.

I have used this method myself when Rollar Blading and though I cannot recommend it, I can swear to its effectiveness. Believe me, when you are sailing (Okay, maybe inching along) the small street in front of your house, the knowledge that you haven't any safety equipment to cushion your fall? Well...you just don't...fall, that is. See, do or die. Either way it works every time.

Speaking of which, I don't think the Park Hosts like me very much. Every time they pass by me on my skates, they laugh (which is not that flattering to begin with) and say with an evil cackle, "Why don't you hook those two dogs up to you for some real speed?" See, not nice at all, especially if you've ever tried to 'hook' my dogs up to anything with wheels connected. Not a pretty picture.

Now some souls baulk at this method and try to reason with those embarking on this rough road. See, that is their first mistake. Assuming there is any reasoning to this. It seems however, as if my oldest grandchild, who is all of three, has decided this life is short enough without adding that sort of philosophy into the mix.

Last month Ken's mom left for heaven and all the cousins and their little ones reunited after several years apart. Now 'Lysie', who is a 'let's all love one another' person, decided to make friends with a little cousin her age who is more a...well, a...three big brothers person. Mia - being the youngest in the family, the only girl and with three rough, red headed older brothers - came into the world as a 'do, or die' sort. I don't think it was even an option. This way of existing was foreign to my grandchild. She is, after all, the oldest and nurturer of all she sees. I think you can see the problem.

Anyway, after an hour or so, she ventured sweetly, "Why don' t we play kitty cats?" No doubt picturing soft gray kittens with pink ribbons tied daintily around their necks.

To which the petite blonde answered back just as sweetly, "Okay."

Then something strange came over the small cousin. Years of ' to do or die' mentality rose it's ugly head. To Lysie's horror, the once before pleasant girl narrowed her eyes, bared her even white teeth, and then threw hands overhead as she roared..."Raawww" in a horribly deep voice.

Shocked, Lysie jumped back, eyes wider than the rest of her face and immediately shook her head madly, saying quickly, "No, no, I meant NICE kitties."

Needless to say Mia was picturing a kitten of a different sort. The lion taming sort that is. Whoops.

But regardless if you embrace this philosophy or not, be wary. There are those around you who do. Even Dallas seems to possess a few of them. One man told me while fishing at the pond, that there was one part of Dallas he was a little afraid to be driving in. See, they have this problem. Keeping manhole covers from being stolen. Now, not being familiar with the area I, like my grandchild, thought why in the world would someone steal manhole covers? I even laughed, picturing people sneaking around in bugler masks and high tech equipment to steal…manhole covers. Pretty funny.

The man however turned serious and shook his head gravely. "They are using them to armor their cars against drive by shootings." This idea was definitely one of those 'do or die' things. Except, I kept thinking that I guess I am not a true 'do or dier'. I only flirt with the philosophy once in awhile. Because if it had been me? I would have moved.

Two Weddings and a Birthday

I think I shall title this stage of life, "the travels of a middle age mom"...or as I like to call it, "My life is not my own".

I remember when my sweet girls were little. I would gather them up in my lap for stories, take long walks discovering butterflies and spend days totally immersed in trying to make a difference in their young lives. Everyone said the time was short so not to waste it. And I didn't. But, I did plan what I would do once they grew up. I went to college and started writing. Everyday I would go into the post office of a dear friend and she would say, "So what are you going to be now Tammy?" I would always laugh because everyday it was something totally different.

But I never imagined in a million years that by the time my girls were grown and gone what I would be is...let's see...a wedding planner (the only experience being my own), an advisor (about such things as how do I know I am in love, and other equally impossible questions), counselor (Entailing long tearful end of the world conversations in which I have no idea what they are talking about), nanny (there is a reason God gives little ones to the young) and a funeral consultant (for all I knew some somber person in black magically put these together).

No. I found out that it is expected of us brave souls who have climbed that infamous forties hill and over – to be the ones in charge. And if truth be told, very few of us have a clue what we are doing. We're just really good bluffers. Take my friend Brenda. She is what I call, a bonefide crafty person. She could make pharaoh's palace out of a couple of pipe cleaners and foil. Pretty amazing. I have seen her type in the park. Are they out hiking the trails, swimming, basking in the sun? Nope. They are the ones sitting atop the wood chips with plastic baggies sifting through the masses of debris looking for cedar. Weird.

So if anyone could do a wedding, Brenda could. Only something happened. Probably surprises like her daughter requesting hand dipped strawberries for two hundred guests. Whatever it was, she definitely was not thinking properly. For one thing she actually asked me to help. A sure sign of insanity. I, not being a crafty person, told my family confidently, "I'll be back in a couple of hours". Nine hours later I was dipping strawberries, decorating tables, and racing around lighting candles. I never did see Brenda, the garter thrown or the rest of my family. I was too busy running in and out of the kitchen. It was crazy.

I thought maybe things would go smoother if I were simply a guest. Wrong. Sounds good except being of the middle age mind set there is a rule somewhere that you can not simply go to anything, but must kill several birds with one stone. You know the mentality. We certainly have our share of people at the park that fit this bill. They are the campers that show up mostly in big groups. Music. Games. People laid out everywhere. They call this madness a family reunion. I generally call it Chaos. And you can most always pick out those who are in charge. They are middle aged, with a faraway look in their eyes, mumbling constantly under their breath about lists and who's in charge of what. Oh, yeah. And they are usually arguing profusely with their spouse.

Well, I am no better. Let's see. In one three day weekend, I decided to drag the girls to Slitterbaun, go to the outlet mall, attend a wedding, and spend the night with old friends. If that weren't enough, Ken even tried to pack one day of school in for good measure. All I can say is we were gone three days and slept four when we got back.

Finally, there was the 'birthing'. My second grandchild.

See, we grandparents have a rep. The kids love us and we adore them. And so we find it fairly easy to entertain them and reread a story forty eleven times without throwing up. Because I will let you in on a little secret…we don't have to do it everyday…or even all day. Yep. It's a piece of cake. Or at least it was until the birthing.

I should have been warned. I see grandparents all the time out here taking their grandchildren camping. I always laugh. Because at the first of the weekend, I see them smiling and fishing together. But by the end of the weekend, I notice the listless bodies of worn out grandparents slumped in lawn chairs as happy children bound around them in limitless expression.

Yep. That was me at Kami's.

So do I have any words of wisdom for all you souls out there reaching middle age? Sure…do what the rest of us do…remember to rotate your tires.

White Men Can't Dance

Ken and I can't dance. Well, at least together. We start out all hopeful like, and then before you know it, our dance resembles more a tug of war over power than the graceful act you see on Dancing With The Stars. Our knees and toes end up so banged up that I am beginning to wonder if we are actually dancing or merely fighting to Floyd Cramer's "The last date". Our attempts at dancing make it seem more like "The Last Stand". Sigh. To say the least, this was not the way I imagined it. Nevertheless, I am determined (or as others call prefer to call it, stubborn); I refuse to give up on my dream of dancing with my husband. Which is why I came up with the brilliant idea to drag him to a dance lesson. This only created more confusion, as I seem to have an attention problem.

Frantically I will whisper, as I tug on his hand and step on his toe, "Are we on two or one?" To which Ken after running into me once again since I have stopped mid-stride hisses (and not romantically I might add), "Tammy, two. How hard can that be?" Then looking down, he stares straight into my face and he starts counting…out loud. This of course does no good. Now I am panicking about whether we are going forward or backwards or turning or…I think you get the picture. Sometimes you just have to waltz away. Or walk, as the situation may warrant.

Jonas experienced one of those times recently…not dancing, but having to walk away. He still is shaking his head a bit over the whole experience. See, it was one of those scorching, sun beating down on you, terribly bad, sticky days. To put it simply, it was hot. As he was passing a through the parking lot checking for illegal entrants, he noticed a movement in one of the shiny black vehicles. Worried he walked over and peeked inside. There sitting on the seat was the cutest puppy you could ever hope to squeeze.

He sat there in misery, weak and panting looking up at Jonas in pleading trust. Jonas was mad enough to spit. He took a deep breath to calm down his churning stomach, and then made for the swimming hole.

He 'excused' his way through a sea of people, but eventually found his prey. The man and his wife where happily frolicking in the cool lake as their puppy lay in the sweltering heat of the black car. It was enough to aggravate most people, even someone as easy going as Jonas. Trying to remain polite, but firm he asked the man to go back and get his dog out of the hot car. The man bowed up, his chest thrust forward and he bellowed back that nothing was wrong with his dog and he had 'cracked' the window.

Now Jonas was getting a little riled. Still, he suggested politely that if it was so fine in the car why didn't he sit for fifteen minutes inside and find out for himself. The man did not appreciate Jonas' suggestion and started carrying on even more. Finally, Jonas won the argument and the man (not exactly in the best of moods) reluctantly went back to check on his dog. There was only one little problem.

The dog had disappeared. The man glared over at Jonas, whose eyes were as big around as saucers. "What happened to my dog?"

Confused and not sure how to answer that question he looked around through the windows once more...nope, the dog had plumb disappeared. Weird. But just as Jonas was going to say he didn't know what had happened to the little feller' well, this yelping, barking sound started up. Which would not have been a problem had the barking, yelping sound not been coming from the back of Jonas's truck. Not a good thing.

Hands up in denial, Jonas started shaking his head, "I did not take that dog out of your car." The only problem being - it was out of his car and in the back of Jonas' truck. The man was livid. Shouting about breaking and entering, violating his rights ect...he commenced his tirade before snatching up his dog and leaving the park and a very befuddled Jonas staring after him. That was when Jonas noticed the two smiling game wardens. They lifted a hand in greeting. Which made Jonas a little suspicious.

Seems they observed another man come by, see the problem of the expiring puppy, and without a moment's hesitation opened the door and rescued the puppy by plopping it into the back of Jonas' truck. Now why they chose to remain silent, just watching the show unfold? Well, it was funny.

Yep, sometimes you just have to walk away.

My sister has this friend, Julie and the longer she stays married, the more toys she seems to accumulate. Boy, would I love to go over to her house. She has a trampoline, a four-wheeler and I don't know what else. Well, the other day she said her husband came home with this dirt bike. Fun. And of course being Julie she wanted to take a ride on the back. So, lost in motorcycle land they raced about on their property, free, unhampered, young and alive. Before long they found themselves sailing along the perimeter fence they shared with a neighbor, who loved dogs. Or so it seemed. He must have at least four that I know of. Anyway, the dogs were running alongside on the other side of the fence, snarling, barking and trying to take them down.

All this commotion was lost to her husband as he bounced along in happy ignorance. Julie is a little more grounded. She noticed the dogs alright, but there was that nice fence separating them from her...that is until one of the pack took a flying leap and cleared it. Horrified speechless, Julie watched as the dog barely broke stride and came straight for them. In a quiet choked voice, she whispered, "Go faster Russell." He slowed to make a corner. The dog did not. After all, boys hate to be told what to do.

The dog gave a wicked grin and sped up. This time she jerked on Russell's sleeve, "Faster. Go faster."

He just ignored her, but did open it up a little more. Maybe now she would stop nagging him. The dog not worried why his good fortune, took advantage of Russell's rebellion. He was now at Julie's heels, snarling and snapping. Victory was nearly his. However, Julie wasn't ready for defeat yet. Gone was the meek, gentle woman he had married as she hit at him and yelled, "I said go faster that dog is going to take us down!"

Looking back in surprise, Russell gunned it, leaving the poor disappointed dog in the dust. Yep, come to find out he never even saw that dog until she yelled at him. Sad but true. Then again it wasn't exactly his ankle that dog intended to latch hold of either. That makes all the difference in the world. See, sometimes you just have to ride away when your wife is telling you to, even if you can't see the danger yourself.

Husbands call this nagging, but we wives? Well, we call it...watching your back.

Maybe that is why even if you want to make a thing work, there comes a time when we all have to just waltz, walk, or ride away. After all not everything has to have an explanation. And to tell you the truth, not everything does.

Wood Duck Boxes, And Other Reasons Couples Fight

I love my husband dearly, don't get me wrong, but I cringe every time I hear the words, "Honey, I need your help for a minute."

To begin with, my husband would not be asking unless he had exhausted all other options.

Secondly, well, men and women do not speak the same language. And herein lies the problem.

I could be waving my hands frantically around my head as my husband continued backing the trailer into a tree. Only to be told I hadn't given him the proper signal. I didn't even know there were right and wrong signals when it came to panicking.

Which brings me to my story.

We have many kinds of birds out here at the park. To name a few there are redbirds, bluebirds and ducks. We even have had some very special wood ducks fly into the park this winter.

Hoping to entice them to stay, we managed to acquire some wood duck boxes. The only drawback was where the boxes had to be placed.

You get it. In the middle of the water.

This is not only a difficult talk, but also doing it from a small boat makes it near impossible.

For one thing, what does the sentence, "hold the boat still," mean exactly?

In girl language it translates–drives the paddle into the mud, closes eyes and hangs on, as said husband pounds the pole into the bottom of the pond.

I would tell you what it means in boy language, but apparently I don't know.

But, I did notice the employees standing on the edge of the bank watching, with big grins on their faces. Which should have been my first warning something was up.

Well, I held the boat.

It shot forward. Ken grabbed onto the pole in an effort to keep from being pitched out. Let's just say, he wasn't very happy.

The employee's grins were widening.

Again, Ken repeated, with a little more aggravation... "Hold the boat still."

As if repeating the same sentence over again would clear it up for me.

I replaced the paddle, only more firmly into the mud and pulled my body up tight against it. The boat jerked backwards. But, Ken was ready this time and quickly dropped back into the boat.

He was shouting. The employees laughing. And me, well, I was glaring. By this time I no longer liked ducks of any kind, especially wood ducks.

Once more he repeated to hold the boat still. And this time the boat went in circles. But at least it was around the pole. So, he drove the box in and gave me a satisfied grin. Before adding, "one more to go."

Let's just say things went downhill from there. Holding boats still and driving in duck boxes from a boat are not talents that improve with practice. Finally, amidst much shouting, laughing and advice from the bank, the deed was done. And I learned a valuable lesson that day.

There are some things, like duck boxes that couples should stay clear of, or at least hire an interpreter.

By the way, the wood ducks love the boxes.

I, on the other hand, have not been asked to help with the awful task again. I think that's for the best, don't you?

Author stuff:

Tammy Watson

The author is married to Ken Watson who works for Texas Parks and Wildlife, when he is not slaying dragons. She enjoys hiking the Davis Mountains where she now lives, and any other adventure her husband takes her on. She has written several books and was published in the The Wills Point Chronicle, as well as the Tawakoni Guide. To check out other books by this author visit her web site at www.tammywatson.com .